Redwood Writers
2020 Poetry Anthology

And Yet

Les Bernstein and Fran Claggett-Holland
Co-editors

Skye Blaine and Susan Gunter
Editorial Assistants

Linda L. Reid
Board Liaison

An anthology of poetry
by Redwood Writers
A branch of the
California Writers Club

Redwood Writers 2020 Poetry Anthology:
And Yet

Editors
Les Bernstein and Fran Claggett-Holland

ISBN: 978-0-9977544-7-6

Book design
by Jo-Anne Rosen
Wordrunner Publishing Services

Front cover art
by Linda Loveland Reid

Back cover art
by Rebecca Smith

Published by Redwood Writers Press
PO Box 4687
Santa Rosa, California 95402

Measuring the Dark

in the dark
when the heavens emptied
and stars restless and roaming
ignited bright white light
with no reflection
shimmering the edges
abstractions fell
as geometries of
attention wavered
between the mind
and the heart

rendered to a human scale
the perceived universe
like a quarter moon
insisted on keeping
the mind's minimal light
awake through the absence
of all it once knew

how do we measure
on these too bright
too illuminated nights
in our fragile vessel
the dark engendered
hard longings of soul

within our smaller perimeter
the heart's valiant efforts
may fizzle and wilt
and yet
a pilot light
glows
warm and steady

— Fran and Les

Contents

And Yet

Introduction

The world of dew
is the world of dew.
And yet, and yet—
    —"Haiku" (1819) by Issa

And yet, like Issa's world of dew, it is so much more! It is your book, a book you will want to keep; it is a book of poems about life, about what we think about life, about all the aspects of life as we live it day by day. It is a book written by some experienced poets, who know how to write what they think and feel. It is a book written by some novices, willing to try their hands at poetry. It is written by a community of writers who share their love of expression through poetry.

If you are one of the writers who have a poem, or two or three, in this book, you will want to keep it close, but you will also want to give it away—to family members, to friends. You will always recognize it because it has a very special cover: a painting of a woman, at the end of a party, perhaps, or the end of a day. She may have had a luminous time, relaxing in happy exhaustion. She may have wanted to find a place to be alone. She may just be tired and want a few minutes of peace and quiet. We don't know. If we ask the artist, Redwood Writers' own Linda Reid, she might have yet a different answer to how we see this woman. But her interpretation is not the only "right" one. She has painted this woman, yes, but now this woman is ours.

It is the same with poems. You will read a poem one way; another person may read it differently. You may like one poem better than another, but your friend may read them in a totally different way, depending on his or her own experiences. Everything we read or write will be interpreted by what we have lived and known in our own lives.

That's another thing; poets who spend time honing their craft are also great readers of poetry and have read and learned from other published poets. Poets find value in working with other poets in a group, learning from each other.

The editors congratulate all the poets whose work appears here. We hope you will read this book over and over. And we hope that you will write and write and write. ... and share poems you love and poems you have written.

> The world of poetry
> is the world of poetry,
> And yet, and yet
>
> with love, Fran

And Yet

for the poets

bonobos use symbols to communicate
border collies know 1,000 words
dolphins have a rudimentary number sense
crows make sophisticated tools
elephants recognize themselves in mirrors
reptiles have their insanely good looks
resembling a bloated kielbasa with dentures
the naked mole rat runs forward
and backward at the same pace
if their mate is unattractive
the zebra finch unwilling to propagate
lays smaller unsurvivable eggs
the bower bird enjoys decorating
with flowers and bright colors
no plaid is involved
in habitat of white page void
the intrepid Redwood Writer
exhibits concentrated industry
welcomes words shaken loose
that rush to the margins
and lay claim to
the whimsy and ineffable beauty
of everyday
life

with love, Les

Acknowledgments

We extend our gratitude to Redwood Writer volunteer proofreaders Susan Gunter and Skye Blaine; to our book design genius and guru Jo-Anne Rosen, and our meticulous webmaster Joelle Burnett. We thank our jack of all trades, answerer of all questions and front cover artist, Linda Loveland Reid. We also extend a special thanks to our back cover artist Rebecca Smith. So many poets have made this book possible: our thanks to them and to the Redwood Writers Board of Directors for supporting this project.

Redwood Writers
Award of Merit Poets

Judy Anderson

Pamela Heck

Louise Hofmeister

Jon Jackson

Robert Shafer

Poets of Merit

The editors are proud to announce this year's Award of Merit Poets. This designation is given to poets whose submission of five poems showed a special quality, demonstrating many of the particular techniques of poetry—imagery, concrete details, rhythm and often, rhyme, used either traditionally or nontraditionally, but always to enhance the essential purpose of their poems. In some cases, these poets exhibited substantial improvement over their previous submissions, testimony to their continual work on the craft of poetry. We are happy to congratulate this year's merit winners.

Judy Anderson

elegies in blue

1

blue eyed mother
blue eyed babies
barefooted children
with marshmallow faces
blue-gray fish from the depths
of blue water daydreams
blue moon harmony
in minor key
today, my own
blue eyed wonder
at the likeness of sky
and your pale eyes
framed in death's still life

2

driving hwy. 1
blue arc of earth
tide pushing inland
blue-gray whale blows
a blue tinged rainbow
resists the pull
of the deep essential blue
is beached

what are we to do but sing the beauty

3

doves coo a blue song
blue flowers frame the blue door
she was sunflower strong
now, her eyes a soft focus blue, gone

is their fire blue spark
still, she stops the boy at the door

holds his attention, *five minutes*
no more, she says then drifts

along the blue shore of not quite life
and not quite death, *so blue*, she says

Judy Anderson

gloaming

we huddle together, arm in arm, family and friends
stories and laughter still ringing in the hush

in the gloaming, a conspiracy of ravens
cracks the silence

the old bear lumbers into the orchard feasting
on fallen fruit—bounty we share

pies cooling on the sill, the smell of apples and
    cinnamon filling the air
hungry as bears, we whisper

night falls and one by one
stars glitter into view

I think of horses, how their goldenrod teeth
crunch an apple, how I learned to hold

my hand out flat, how I loved
the man who taught me

how horses smell fear
how they greet each other nuzzling

nose to nose, how they mourn
the passing of their mate

to dust

weeks after the fires
tiny columns of smoke still rise
a light rain falls   too late

embers hiding in debris sizzle
the way my hair sizzled in the blaze
eyelashes and brows singed and brittle   break

when touched   we all do

massive oaks fallen   vanish under our feet
     phantom trees   dissolving to dust

sculptures of ash   memory of trees
   memory of home

dust

for june

clouds of dust rising
your bare feet stomping in the soft earth
to a rhythm only you knew

sheltered under a fragrant pine, I watch you
tapping my feet in unison not knowing then
how brief your dance would be

your hair falling across your shoulders
catching sunlight and your eyes
the color of dawn

half your young age
my maturity as elusive as your dreams
I grasp your hands we twirl
what could I know then of your pain

why I collect feathers

my mother returned to me as a bird
an ordinary bird, all of a single color
or so it seemed in the flurry of wing beat
her plumage befitting a pain-dulled life

yet so easily she maneuvered walls
of grief and anger, the lifelong
obstacles between us, shifting

hovering close, did she whisper?

she was gone in an instant
tipping her wing as if to wave
brilliant feathers floating
all around me

Pamela Heck

He will not be my "friend"

He calls that word the stop sign
a woman holds before a man
to halt the journey
before a step is taken.
A milder "F" word,
if you will.

He is not my lover,
though that I will consider
at some future time
if all goes well.
Until then,
words are just semantics,
and "stop" is just a resting place.

But I tell you now,
if we are lovers,
on that day
he must also be my friend,
though I will say "amigo"
if he likes.

Marking Time

With trees, God draws rings
around their hearts—
circular signs of the ages
etched upon inner pages.

With women, God draws lines
upon their faces—
inner secrets posted
in public places.

Roadside Reflection

(dedicated to Kay Ryan)

Splayed upon the road, a deer,
whose frenzied leap from there to here
turned destination into destiny.
Testament that sudden ends
begin with simple choices.

Had she but raced ahead,
or tarried more,
she might have thwarted fate—
collision's course averted
by a single step.

Rhyme No More!

Rhyming is passé,
or so they say,
and wanting
to be recognized
as serious,
rather than spurious,
I try to refrain.

No matter that I find rhyme
juicy and delicious;
I bow to the officious guardians
of modern verse.
Rhyme no more!

What is Wordsworth worth
if he won't stop rhyming?
I advise him to forget the rhyme
and concentrate on timing.

Stop teaching
"Stopping by Woods
On a Snowy Evening."
It's deceiving.
Children will grow up
thinking rhyming is OK,
and then, rhyming
will NEVER go away.

Pamela Heck

Less Than Me

Wrapped in white sheets like a spectral bride,
I lay warm and cozy by his side.
Nested like spoons beneath the covers,
we weren't in love, but we were lovers…
each cast adrift by a failed romance,
and drawn together, it seemed, by chance.
So, it wasn't love. Well, no, not quite,
though we held each other in the night.
I watched the darkness ebb away,
as dawn slipped in and turned to day.
Then words, like stones, tossed across the bed,
"Soon it will be too late," he said.
"Too late for what?" was my reply.
"Too late for me," and then a sigh.
"You're too creative and much too smart.
I'm pulling back to save my heart.
Love is something I can't espouse.
I want a woman to keep my house—
to care for me, not some career.
I can't afford to keep you, dear."
The warmth I felt moments ago,
melted away like an early snow.
Now, I can't say he broke my heart.
I mean, who dumps you for being smart?
Certainly, someone who wanted less,
and that wasn't me, I must confess.
I got the gift of being free.
I'm sure he found someone less than me.

After Limbo

In the collapsed heap
of time spent waiting
for an answer,
not knowing offers pale solace.

When shadows frame our days
we say
some evidence of light remains.
We stage our best distractions.

Then news comes
and we start again—
fall back into our old
routines.
Forgotten is
the freeze, the lull
that kept our lives at bay.

Unless, instead
we hear the words
that pierce the heart
and slap the flank
of our high-strung mortality.

That's when we lose our feet
and land where time ticks louder—
That's when we lock our knees
and sleep while standing.

Louise Hofmeister

Summer's End

These are the days of river cool
when summer dust
streaks swimmer's feet.
A filigree of
Queen Anne's lace
trims every ditch and road.

These are the days of gravensteins
of zuchs and cukes for pickling
and lavender hung in rafters.
While all around us roses fade
pink trumpets blare,
as though to show the way.

In yards tomatoes drop and melt
beneath the laden vines
In kitchens, fingers, purple-dyed
flute crusts for berry pies
And so I will pick and slice these things,
make sauces and arrangements.

But for whatever I preserve
and for each moment held,
I cannot slow the growing pace,
but note the growing rumble-
as everywhere days gallop into Fall.

Pacemaker

Awake again
and hope revived,
they shimmy with relief
like silver creatures cast back
which, once freed,
will twist and flip
securing their release-

an exit that to all appears
a mighty jump for joy.

By the grace of intervention,
some amazing new device,
comes a save that of itself
shrugs one closer to divine.

"So she's returned to working out..."
"He's bicycling again..."
"They're back at doubles tennis every day." —

It seems they've stuck a landing
where nothing more remains
than without regret or stumble
to replay an old design.

And what about the measure
of life in terms of motion
leads me to think
that cannot be enough?

The gift of borrowed time
calls for rapt eyes and keen attention
to seek and sound the contours
of its promise.

Past the hour of celebration
on the threshold of the new
don't forget
the circling fin of darker outcomes-
for the leap without reflection
finds no light.

.

Sun Again

After the tractor mower
had groomed those glistening rows
a clan of robins
pow-wowed
all through the churn
and beaming green.

Emerging with
damp feathers
from days of dodging drips
and nights of hunkering down
their hops and dips
appeared a juicy jig.

All hail to the trifecta
of warming light,
and softened earth,
and relocating worms!

Those robins did
a bang up job of
ushering in the Spring

Who cared if it was early?
Who cared if it was false?

Written on the Wall

The laureate of Cleveland Street
has lost her train of thought
lifetime subscriber to the Muse
whose words cannot be caught

Quotes saved her for a little while
her go-to potluck dishes
But when she summons even those
elude her recall wishes

Not long since she could find a thread
on pausing for diversion
but often now those birds once flown
are over the horizon

These days the Muse keeps taunting her
as she keeps slipping stitches
Her only respite now are songs
but even those have hitches

The laureate of Cleveland Street
does not have far to go
before she comes to where she
doesn't know she doesn't know

The Tale of Noah

Imagine Noah at the end of the Ice Age.
The glaciers are melting, seas rising.
Atlantis has gone underwater.
Civilizations are drowning, or learning to swim.
Everything is changing, new maps drawn.
His sons report warmer weather
All over the known world.

An ocean of water sits high above the valley.
Its icy lip thinning as danger looms.
He wants to save his animals from the flood.
So, he builds a boat that will only float.
His daughters report dying crops.
Men all around call him mad.

One day, the ice rim cracks, the frigid water
Sitting poised, ready to fill the void.
It is time. He leads his animals
Into the massive zoo, meticulously tailored.
His men report imminent disaster.
The ice rim cracks again.

At the foot of the valley is a stone wall, miles long,
Solid, firm, two hundred yards high.
It was made by men to keep strangers out.
But today, it will also keep the water in.
His animals report anxious dis-ease.
And the flooding begins.

The first torrent slams the heavy door shut.
The huge vessel spins like a top.
Men are thrown overboard into violent waves.
The border wall holds, the village is destroyed.
They all hear reports of snapping trees.
As the vessel lifts and floats.

For days they drift ever closer to the wall.
The new lake breaches, creating waterfalls.
Outside, all see the bobbing ship high above,
Expecting it to fall, come crashing down.
Soldiers report evacuations.
All hangs tense and beautiful.

Finally, a tunnel through the wall gives way.
The drain begins, a new river rushes out.
What was old washes away, destroyed.
But the huge wall stands firm, strong.
The shamans report sunny skies
As everything changes.

Weeks later, the water is only slightly down.
The boat is grounded on the valley's arm.
All is intact, no one else has died.
Noah finally opens the door as silence abounds.
His wife reports that she is pregnant.
And the sky is a new strange blue.

The Fifth Glass

This afternoon, my ex-wife came to visit,
With her new wife - and we all
Set up a table on the back porch.

We were having wine and cheese
Purchased on our long trip,
A big loop locally - and we all, somehow,
Thought we were one wine glass short.

When we talked about it later,
We all agreed ... And, yes, they had told me
To bring the glass out, and, yes, I did.
Like we were one glass short.

And, yet, there were only four of us.
In attentive silence, we examined
That fifth glass, the one that all of us
Had said was missing ...

Then, we clinked our glasses, and we
Shared that wine amongst ourselves,
A good one, from a Calistoga winery.
And we all said ...

Well, she's not here, anyway ...

Jon Jackson

Nothing is Far in Mayreau

The womb is unnamed as you begin,
Steep hills are the forward path, but
There is an easier one behind you,
Though you'll never see the keys there.

The oppressive heat is like the palm
Of a hand standing between you
And the goals you have chosen. No wind
To lift you, only scattered shade.

You look up and think of what they say,
"Nothing is far in Mayreau," but,
Why not turn and stay near the water?
You don't really need to see the keys.

Or do you? So you climb, step-by-step,
And each peak you reach leads only
To a turn in the road, and the next
To another. But still you climb.

At the top, you pause to consider,
And look back down the way you came.
You trusted too long in raw fortune.
Your goal requires an active will.

Back down the hill is a Catholic church.
The grounds offer a better shade.
A bird-like music flows through the trees,
A stony path winds past the door.

So, it can't be far now, can it?
Through the trees, under a blue sky,
The palm now protects you from behind.
Here is the garden, and the keys.

From start to peak, to the garden path,
With one mistake along the way,
It's true, nothing is far in Mayreau.
You simply have to find a way.

Eve

In our mythology, our literature, our world,
There is at least one woman
Who never experienced the loss of her mother.
And that would be Eve.

I say "at least" because
The same would be true of Lilith.
But, that's another story, more hidden,
And not Official, as it were.

Not just the loss.
The experience of a mother.
Our unconscious memories of womb,
Our infant's recollection of face.

To say nothing of how she fed us,
Raised us, taught us, created us.
As we flailed through adolescence,
Repeating her own personal mistakes.

Our rebellion and disavowal,
Our rejections of her, her life experience.
How it all came together, one way or another,
And we finally saw her, the woman that she is.

Perhaps too late? Or maybe not?
But, Eve never knew her mother,
Never had a mother, any mother.
She was the only one, the only woman.

Imagine having to figure that out
On your own. No one before you
To tell you it was normal, alas.
And tell you to be proud of who you are.

Showtime

Are we ready to step aside
And let the other speak?
Through our children?
Through the ones
We've said don't matter? Through the ones that say
"MeToo" to the vacant void?

Through the ones that die every day,
Everywhere, around the world,
To whom we say, "We support you!"
As they fall, and they say
"No, you never will," and
"No, you never have"?

Are we ready to let
Another species awaken us
To things we've always
Said we believe?
The ones who say, "You hypocrites!"
"You who settled for
Soft beds, and something
Supposedly normal"?

Are we ready to say, "Enough!"
As others have always said,
Time and again, with no credibility?
Those whom we say we must help,
But never do, not really?

Can we give up our comfortable lives,
Or dominion? We thought what we did
So long ago made us worthy of it.
Are we willing to lay down ourselves,
Our reputations, our careers,
Our safety? All on the line?
Are we willing to take a stand,
At last, after so many years,
When we thought we won
Back then. We'd done our part.
There was nothing more.

Are we?

If not, then, you know,
Our children will die,
Our spouses demeaned,
Our dark selves will lie in the streets,
Dead, as thousands spit and sink
Into poverty and shit.
And you. You will go on
In your comfortable life
Until, one day, you
Are brought down, too.

Believe me. Please.
Our large work was never finished.
It has, again, been
Thrown to the ground.
And it will happen again,
Unless you wake up now.

Unless you say, "Enough!"
Now!
At what is in front of you.

Or don't. Your decision.
I'll honor that. But, then,
I won't be there to help you
When your life is adrift
And you need me.
Because I will be gone,
One way or the other.

Nicotine Baby

Father
was
a parking lot attendant.

Mother
just a waitress.

Father
smoked cigarettes.

Mother
smoked cigarettes.

The good dose of nicotine
I got,
when I fed at mother's breast,
jangled my nerves a lot,
I couldn't wait for another shot.

Father
never held me
close to his chest.
He thought I was
too different
from the rest, too far
from the best.
He shared
only
his cigarette smoke.

Curls
and clouds of smoke,
floated down,
from my parent's
toxic, tobacco toke.

Tears
flooded
my eyes.
A raspy cough,
burst
from
my baby throat.

Still,
I felt
Mother's
love emote.

Father
loved
only his cigarettes.

So what,
my clothes
had burn holes,
and ash stains.

So what,
cigarettes
killed
my mother.

So what,
cigarettes
killed
my father.

I continue
to dream,
about those days.

Mother
held me close.

We shared
her cigarette smoke.

Children and War

Profiteers,
from the
worldwide war industry,
ignore
the presence
of the
helpless,
frightened,
children.

The children
try to climb
over greed
and hate's
restraining wall,
but

their shoddy shelters
and their fragile minds
collapse,
during another
merciless
war.

The children's
small bodies
lay in a mangled,
bloodied
mess,
their heartless
killers

once again,
refusing
to care
and desist.

The innocent
children's deaths,
from public discourse,
quickly
fade away,
though
around the world
the war makers
continue

to bomb
and slay.

The
ruthlessly
slaughtered
children,
only wanted
one last chance,

to live,
to laugh,
to play.

Horse

Race with the wind,
unrestrained
and uninhibited.

Dazzle with your speed,
charm with your beauty.

Nostrils flared with fire,
thick mane flows free.

Tail proudly held aloft,
four hooves defy gravity.

I'm entranced
and bedeviled,
by your indomitable
spirit.

I'm impressed by
and in fear,
of your great strength.

You radiate warmth
all around,
yet you shiver
at an admirer's touch.

Suppress your
inborn instinct
to recklessly flee
from everything.

You find it difficult
to rely on humans,
but there is no wild herd
to escape to.

A harsh hand releases
your flood of fear,
a soft touch
soothes your horse.

Gentleness
usually doesn't work,
with hyenas,
piranhas,
or wasps,
but lightness
will bring
a happy response,
from the equine
every time.

Earning your trust
is my goal,
seeing you at peace
is my reward.

Bonding with
your wildness
fulfills
my most fervent
fantasy.

Blue Whale

Largest mammal
on our earth,
man saw only
your dollar's worth.

Victim of greed's
killing notions,
your innocent blood
reddened oceans.

Father,
mother,
infant,
without distinction,
ruthlessly hunted,
nearly to extinction.

Although some
Blue Whales are back,
our environmental
diligence
must not slack.

As humans consume,
and deface,
nature shrivels
and dies apace.

When this earth
is uninhabitable,
distant planets
may not
be compatible.

Earth Was Dying

I hiked along
a potholed highway

I saw above me,
endless pollution

I saw below me,
littered valleys

I saw before me,
a billion tree stumps

I saw behind me,
a vast junkyard

All around me,
Earth was dying.

I wept as I trekked
past oil-soaked beaches
mountains of garbage
rivers of chemicals
oceans of plastic
fields of wildlife corpses

All around me,
Earth was dying.

The sun was blazing
streams were drying

flowers were wilting
forests were burning
smoke was rising
embers were spreading
ashes were falling

All around me,
Earth was dying.

I stumbled along
the conqueror's highway,
fulfilling
my Manifest Destiny.

Nobody could ever stop me.

Nobody could ever turn me back.

Only I could stop
my destructive ways.

All around me,
Earth was dying.

And Yet

An Absence of One

for Karina

the scent of burning beeswax
a canning jar upon the kitchen table
where someone has arranged
a clamorous bouquet of mustard flowers
from the field behind your cottage
purple thistle heads exploding
woodfern fiddleheads unscroll
heralding an early spring

you are not here
not here to greet me.

Great sadness attends us
as we gather round your death
to sing the sacred songs
we once performed together:

Iavnana, a lullaby of roses
Letjat Utki, a lament
Oh, follow the geese in migration,
Shen Khar, a kind of prayer:
you are the fresh young sapling
blooming in paradise
you are the sun
shining all over

all over
so soon

What will become of the guida
you carried from Bulgaria
the one you loved and
worked so hard to master,
the complex fingerings
and how to breathe authentically
filling the goatskin bag with
the warm air of your lungs.
Your reedy skirl never failed
to animate the dancers.

Who will try on your
closetful of costumes now:
extravagance of floral scarves
hand embroidered peasant blouses
flouncy underskirts with lacy hems
dancing shoes with curled toes.

On the dresser, twisted
strands of scarlet beads
nesting with the heirloom
amber necklace your mother
and your mother's mother
used to wear.

Those notebooks piled upon your desk . . .
are they the drafts of memoir
you said you'd share with me

some day
some other day

Today
your face is cool as porcelain,
no trace of pain
that dogged your hours
awake or sleeping
all these many months

We'll never harmonize with you
from this day forward
never join our hands with yours
as we smile into each other's eyes
and take our final bow

Where are you now
my friend
Where will you go
from here

Children of the Farmers' Market

Mardi Gras colors: scarlet, jade
earthy aromas: mushroom and weed,
tikka masala, fistfuls of lavender,
pots of paella, fresh baked bread.

Toddler in pimento leggings,
face adorned with swirls of daisies,
rocks her amply diapered bum
to the heartbeat of a bongo drum.

Three little boys play Peek-a-Boo,
tug at the skirt of a produce stand,
peer from beneath like fugitives
of cauliflower trees and turnip bombs.

Blown in by the wind
that lifts the canopies,
feral progeny storm the alleys,
dodging and darting between the stalls.

A girl in ragged dungarees
shinnies a street sign to the top
waves to her brothers down below
claims the metal with a victory slap.

When did I trade untethered joy
for such a tightly bridled realm:
my packages of perfect berries
tidy display of bottles and jars.

One hand on the money box
in a symmetry of give and take,
I wait for customers to come,
gauging the weight of time until
the shutting down of summer sun.

Mardi Gras colors: scarlet, jade
earthy aromas: mushroom and weed,
tikka masala, fistfuls of lavender,
pots of paella,
fresh baked bread

Confessions of a Wild Child

Don't call me Barbara;
I am Alice antique and flawless
hailed from history's showcase.
Bring me high button shoes,
the flounce and bustle,
whalebone to bind my middle.

No. Call me Sagebrush Sal.
Let me ride a half-broke pony
black hair whipping
across my eyes as I traverse
the high plateaus on sparking hooves.

All around me, clods of dirt explode,
smoke bombs on the asphalt playground.
Pursuing the last of the cowboys,
I tear through the hedge ripping
my satin Christmas jacket.

On a yellow pad with a yellow #2,
I scribble a poem before I sleep.
No boogieman appears tonight
veiled in the shadows of my curtains.
A contraband Madonna porcelain blue
maintains her post outside my window ledge.

". . . Be advised: your daughter, Barbara, is no longer wel-
come in our Campfire Circle. She ties her classmates' shoes
together underneath the table. . ."

Mama
Listen to me
I can't make
their tissue paper flowers.

the green glass bowl

Old friends weigh in
on time-worn couches
old dog shrugs her covers
lifts her head to take us in.
So many of us have come and gone . . .
does she remember how we used to be

> Take a piece of candy
> from the green glass bowl
> ride across living room
> on plumes of peppermint
> take up a customary role
> with inside jokes and tales of woe.
> Let us resume our journey
> down this beaten path.

On paws no bigger than my thumbs
a puppy crawls into my lap,
with clever little claws proceeds to scale
my sweater on his quest for Annapurna.
He looks me in the eye and licks my chin.
Seasoned laughter skids around the room again.

In one another's company,
we occupy old ways of being.
How can we be so different now
and still remain so much the same.

> Take a piece,
> a piece of candy
> from the green glass bowl.

> Save another for the long,
> or the long road home . . .

Wasting Time

How much time in a lifetime
How much consumed in idle moments
Do we begrudge the stasis
between heartbeats,
the marking of time
in airless waiting rooms,
the copious years of sleeping
as if our lives did not
depend on them.

Imagine then, the teller's tale
without its poignant pauses . . .
the tanka deprived of
its room for dreaming,
ascholarlythesiswithoutaspacebar
to allow for meaning.
Contemplate time as a painter
whose boldest strokes
would be devoid of potency without
 the quiet canvas in between.
Observe the negative space.
Honor it.

Count it as time
well spent.

Dust

They thunder into the yard like extinct dinosaurs
Filling up the space
Huge, heavy laden blocks
 Of metal and rubber and dust
Always dust...
My cousins emerge from either side
Jumping from the head of the beast
Slamming the doors
As their feet hit the ground
And the dust
Always that dust haloing around them
Black shadows
Against the sun
Blocking out the light

The coal trucks are back
The boys are home
They make their way into the basement
To shed their clothes like snake skin
Their clothes
Their faces all black with coal dust
Only their eyes smile out
Brown on white orbs

I wait outside that basement door
A fresh picked tomato for each
A salt shaker
And a beer
Each thing covered with a cold,
black coal colored dust
Clinging like peach fuzz

That constant dust we eat
No matter how hard we try to clean
Or mop
Or rub
Or scrub

They come out
My cousins
Laughing
Shaking their heads
Like the hunting hounds baying in their pens
They are wet and clean

The turn my head with one large hand
And reach for the cold, dusty beer bottle with the other

I wait every day for them
I wait for that transformation
From coal dusted blackened men
To the stark tee shirt white of these two
Who slide into the dark womb of the earth
As easily as my feet into my slippers
I wait with that fierce child faith
As if death was not a back drop of this mining town
Where we know
We will, one day
Be a part of
That this dust we live in

Names

When we see something new,
something new under the sun,
or out there beyond the sun,
we gotta give it a name.
When astronomers saw light
coming from interstellar dust clouds
they named it cloudshine.

Naming started long ago.
According to one account:
"God formed every beast of the field,
and every fowl of the air,
and brought them to Adam to see
what he would call them:
and whatsoever Adam called
every living creature,
that was the name thereof."

Adam's progeny did a lot of naming,
had a thing for the alphabet;
there's over a hundred Zs:
Zephaniah, Zedekiah, Zachariah…

Classy names, like *all* the oldies:
Obadiah, Nehemiah, Jedidiah …
So fine compared to Bob, Bart, or Bret.
No panache, no gravitas.
Not the stature of a Lazarus
nor the durability of a Methuselah.

The writer of Ecclesiastes said,
"There is nothing new under the sun."
Not so. We keep naming them,
though some, like cloudshine,
seem a little clunky to me.

Indian Summer

Frightened by the whip and whirl of frantic fierce winds,
blistering heat dissipates.
Wild winds, catching up dust and leaves,
pulsing, pushing,
sneaking powdery trash inside our homes,

kissed by the breeze, instigate a sneeze,
deflates our days as winter waits for autumn to fall.

Hiss, whoosh, whisper, crackle!
Electrified air hums, flicks, frizzes.
Hair salutes, stands on end, flies in our faces,
blinds our eyes as a red gold sun transmutes the light,
incandescent as the blush of your cheek.

Gratitude gathers in the garden,
a penultimate blast of abundance,
gracefully rejiggers expectations,
a radiant herald, harbinger of hibernation.
Hopeful harridans, we hasten to harvest,
scrambling ahead of impending desiccation or deluge.
Vines shrivel, reveal plump fruit poised for picking
as a weakened sun sucks up vitality,
preparing to pack up for the season,
like vacationers eager to return home,
spent following a frenzied, frolicsome summer.

I Will Listen

to you ramble on
about what you did, and what you
need to do, how your work is going,
who does your hair and
what you had for dinner

just to get to
the heart of it
the thing that makes you sing
and crow
or wail
and writhe —
the story that haunts you
when no one is looking
the memory that mists your eyes
the longing that could kill
you all by itself.

I will wade through used tissues
I will offer up my body to be misted with gossip
I will laugh at your jokes
I will hold a sign that says I will work for food
and wait a hundred years
until you look me in the eye
and tell me something real

When Mrs. Goodman Said Yes

When Mrs. Goodman said yes
and opened herself to him

When he came in the door
after work and set down his lunchbox

When he wanted her,
not with wooden groping
but saying "Oh, my Sadie, my Sadie"
and she felt his thick hand
behind her waist pulling her to him

When Mrs. Goodman said yes
and her sensible shoes, her dress
and baking apron
were heaped on the floor by the bed,
his overalls flung

When puffs of flour floated
in the shaft of sunset light through
the bedroom window
and she breathed in his smell
of oil and man

She thought to herself,
"Now supper can just wait."

Margaret Barkley

Live as though you are light

Are you a being of light now inhabiting flesh?
or are you a series of chemical reactions
causing muscle to move?

All of us are pieces of meat
made living —

Your body, my body, the body of the cat
walking by with her tail alert

Either everything is holy,
or nothing is holy

Quick — which is it?

Either way, your body will someday wear
the face that reminds us of you, but isn't

Poetry of Pie

Sift the flour, she says.
I have always skipped this step
but she is the master and says
sifting will keep it light,
lifts the flour in the deep bowl
with gentle fingers like she is fluffing air.

Then a pinch of salt, just like it sounds,
carried between finger and thumb.
Add butter chopped in pieces
tossed into the flour like rolling the dice,
like the gamble that it is —
the flakiness of crust will depend
completely and forever on your tender touch.

She says this can be done with a pastry cutter,
but fingers work just fine.
She shows us, spreading butter between deft fingertips,
never lingering enough to melt it.
The butter pieces get smaller and smaller,
surrounded by the fluff of flour,
but not merged with the flour,
With my own fingers I can feel it,
this joining but not joining,
till like magic it is a new substance altogether,
still loose like air, but now with the weight of added
 gold.

She shows us how to make a furrow in a circle
like plowing fairy earth,
then sprinkling in water,

we lift and mix with light fingers,
sprinkle more,
then lift and mix again.
More water, I think,
but no — she says.
The secret is knowing when to stop,
before it looks like anything new
but is just starting to be friendly to itself.

Stop and gather it loosely,
like you would a curled-up kitten,
like something just born,
and barely love it into a shaggy shape.
Wrap it and chill for twenty minutes

then hold it again in your hand
and see that it has become
one thing
all on its own,
while you were busy cutting apples
licking cinnamon sugar from your fingers.

With fingertips she strews flour
on the board like snowfall
more on the wooden pin.
She shows us how to roll our new dough,
evenly and from the center, like throwing a pot,
adding flour as needed
till it is a wide circle thin but sturdy
enough to fold, to pick up and move —
a miracle, I think.

Lay this creation in your pie pan — glass is best.
Pile with apples steeped in sugar, lemon, cinnamon
dot with more butter.
Roll a second circle to cover your mountain of fruit

crimp the edges with dancing fingers and thumb
a rippled circumference
joining the dough disks together
so that no oven can tear them asunder
knife prick the top in the shape of apple or heart
and bake it till the smell takes over
your whole life.

Beauty on the Edge

Just before it happened
I heard the sound of wings
Erasing what I thought was mine to hold:

light of lavender,
jasmine after a rain,
helping hands
encouraging words

All distractions hiding harmonies
Just beyond the range of hearing
Not gentle but sounding a harder truth

The stream has an unerring flow
Saying "jump in … let go"
trust
Even over the falls

Forever over the falls

Currency

our lives are
merely currency
change that we spend
hair thins, middle thickens
mind grows rigid
memories grow vivid
new ones we forget

and lines appear
to be read like maps
they tell where we have been
reveal the challenges endured
deep ones reveal suffering
little ones mark joy
long deep ones represent
years of single mindedness
things we should have learned
and perhaps ignored

the dreams we did not realize
are now the moments of regret
the roads we have traveled in miles
the roads wished for in mind
there is no difference at the end

perhaps the outcome
is predetermined
but this is certain
one day
there will be
no more currency to spend

Inevitable

brightness dims
a quick wit slows
intensity wanes
knife edges dull
a boil now simmers
memories murmur
whisper and fade

Apocalypse Soup

liquify
optimism
spirit
hope

add
greed and avarice
religious fanaticism
random acts of terror
wild climate change
natural disasters

heat
to boiling ove
strain
remove
logic
intelligence
compassion

make ready
for packaging
and world wide distribution

add
mandatory warning label
may cause
chronic depression
nausea
restlessness
insomnia
suicidal thoughts

long term exposure
may prove fatal

Henrietta Bensussen

What the Russians Left Behind

Early spring narcissus blooms
hundreds planted by elderly Russians,
dug up, re-planted, among apple, plum,
apricot trees. Roses, weeds. Incense cedar.

We moved into their small house
to make it ours, our nuclear family
of four: husband, a determined
togetherness for children, a home.

By age three the girl took up
housework, not that I taught her
that drudgery, she got it by watching
her mother. She liked cookery. Plus

sewing/quilting/words/travel. College.
Responsibility eventually, how to
manage bills and keep it all going
in spite of everything. A lot like me.

A boy who played in the dirt
with miniature trucks,
planted his own
garden, wandered through a secret
town known to us. Also like me

The dog the father had always wanted.
Polite and patient: a prince who found
himself in a hovel, an acceptance of fate.
A quiet guard, considerate mob boss.

We enlarged the house, adding a deck—lost
the narcissus, and the dog slipped in mud,
so sent to sleep too young, and later,
I left as well, following the children

to college, and into a New World.
Cats, of course, many of them. They arrived,
disappeared as they wished, unlike dogs.
In the cupboard after the Russians had gone

I found a wooden meat cleaver,
left it there for other women to find.

Trick or Treat

ring the bell
and don't get caught
there are monsters
in the basement
quiet as a thought

bracketed by the dark
is life's drift and mystery
nothing but noise
a disposable history

as involuntary as a hiccup
the clock endlessly circles
claims further territory
brooks no reversal

amid sunshine and smiles
a need to masquerade
only so many heartbeats
permit this charade

so trick or treat
and here is the clue
tick tock
tock tick

boo

Come Sit Stay

for Mouse and Matt's Magoo

"Dogs are well known for their ability
to backtrack to a beloved home — or person"

— Clairborne Ray

a departure seen coming
yet sudden as a sneeze
strays to an inevitable story
pulls on the leash
of vertiginous sorrow

you have traveled too far
and I've become untethered
can you
will you
find me
will there be a time
we border and greet
again

will you come
if I whisper your name
in a language
with only
one speaker
left

Bifocals

the psychic said
he had made contact with my mother
she was wearing glasses
large ones
I was sure
she could lose those
in the afterlife
what about her hearing aids
where was she getting batteries
and her diabetic testing supplies
what about dialysis
were there kidney support centers
did she have to watch her salt intake
what about her compression socks
and her thyroid medication
and the tiny little anti-depressant pill
she took
so she wouldn't mind dying
organ by organ
so much

"Bifocals" first appeared in *Oxford Poetry*, 2018

Adab—courtesy

A certain courtesy of heart
"*Adab*" we dervishes say
it's rude to stretch feet
toward the guide in the center

respect for the teacher
is heartfelt and so true
it is seen in the carriage
of our bodies

we kiss the ground
reverent, grateful for its support
each breath imbued with
the name of God

How this offended my atheist dad
yet he showed his own propriety
kindness, respect toward employees
courtliness with his wife

Heart attack took him before I revealed
we walk the same bridge
face the same way
over the same sharp chasm

Ode to the Morning Shower

1987

You, you were the way back
the rush—
drenching, beating, thundering my heart
I lifted my face to the warm cascade
first upward movement out of rage
in months

My friends had grown so tired of me

You offered one small delight
five minutes of warmth, of touch
you flushed away revenge
Because of you, the fig tree
that marked our marriage day
survived my axe

You pummeled me awake—you
you were the way back

Syria

Who protects the babies
bony, big-bellied,
flies sipping their tears?
Toddlers suck their mothers dry
whimper at unfairness
they know as tight belly and thirst

The infant stuffs dusty fingers
in her mouth to quell her need
her bewildered gaze asks
what now

Dysentery? Malaria?
Illness happy to ravage
where hope is gone
How can I reach
this child, or the next,
the next, the next

I, white, with too much to eat
watch the daily desolation
from my chair
pray, donate dollars
it is not enough

Bird Calls for my 70th Birthday

My eyes track
a young hummingbird
luscious
red-headed
fluttering to survive
lured by deep color
odor of sweet pollen
lost in life's scent.

Nearby
a common sparrow
of dull dusty brown
bathes in muddy water
preens ruffled feathers
sings an ancestor song
traps insects
in my wild garden.

I hear an owl shriek
in my neighbor's barn
when darkness comes.
She feasts on
mice and shrews
shares her home
with flying bats
content to live in shadow.

Yet I long to follow
a white-tailed kite
emerging new from the nest
vast blue space before her

no questions
no ancient pain
only a call to fly
high above tall pure pines.

I See You

Synchronicity reigns as
you see fearless children
leap into unknown
spaces shaping your
impulse and intuition

I see you joyfully, playfully
calling each new form forth,
ready to risk a deep unveiling
ready to embrace your essence
ready to live your purpose now

I see you now
standing in the space
of all possibilities with
your power framed in
wisdom being birthed

Upper East Side Sonnet

First you feel the rumble in your feet
Vibration deep and low disturbs your bones
Just a warning mammoth moving tons
Of mass before the burgeoning sound of loud.

Then wind moves the dark detritus
Of tunnel steel and hint of oil to nose
Lore of rodents, seeping damp of rain
To those in suits, cologne, and pantyhose.

Next lights so bright dispel the emptiness
The candid, naked face of beast reveals
Its origin, name and destination clear
As it pulls into the station of your fears.

Opening entrance doors or exits appeal
Far beyond transit, humanity must congeal.

Mother's Day in Suburbia

After orders have been given,
And fresh flowers are placed in the vase,
Complex feelings must be hidden.

Very fine people avoid a tiff,
Take Mom to lunch on Mother's Day
After orders have been given.

At brunch, truthin' and fibbin'
'Bout yards to be cleaned and trees to be pruned
Complex feelings must be hidden.

Very fine people drive deaden
Overburdened asylum-seekers
After orders have been given.

Remove toddlers from the Eden
Of Mami y Papi in tears.
Complex feelings must be hidden.

See detention camps, profit driven
Chain link enclosures cold.
After orders have been given,
Complex feelings must be hidden.

Sprinkle

They sprinkle it on salads as they limit the ballot
wipe their mouths with fine linen as the officers keep killin'
young brothers talking business or average daily walkin'
little boy in a park, young man in walmart talkin'

It's sprinkled 'cross the screen and we get it in our eyes
it's not a gun, it's a phone, it's not a gun, it's just a toy
he's black, not a gun, and he's a man, he's not a boy
it's NOT a gun that a child was waving in a park
it's not a gun, it's a toy, it's a wallet, it's a phone, it's not a . . .

. . . boom bam done can't take the bullets back
. . . boom goes the gavel' nother voter off the ballot
. . . boom bam crack Oscar Grant in the back.

darkness
darkness in the court darkness in the court
… darkness of the heart … darkness of the heart

If what the officer sees is what he believes
and what he believes the officer will see
In "A Talk to Teachers" Baldwin decrees
"I knew enough about life by *this* time
to understand that whatever *you* invent
whatever you project is *you!*"
Collected Essays, page 682.
What's Jimmy Baldwin sayin'
'bout me, 'bout you?

See, it's sprinkled across our screens so it gets in our eyes
it's not a gun, it's a phone, it's not a gun, it's just a toy

he's brown, not a gun, he's just a teen, more than a boy
it was a toy that Andy Lopez was holding in a field

But what officer believes is what he will see
tears and wailing in Santa Rosa indeed
he can't admit what he sees isn't what he believes
she can't admit what she sees isn't what she believes
BUT "It is not permissible that the authors of devastation
should also be innocent. It is the innocence
that constitutes the crime," James Baldwin, page 292,
from "My Dungeon Shook: Letter to My Nephew…"
Fast forward to more "innocence" today
or perhaps it's amnesia:
Poll taxes become Voter ID Laws
Plantations become prisons
Public education turns to public private partnerships
Redlining becomes subprime mortgage loans
economic inequality re-segregates the country
alleviates that "do I have to *deal with you* feeling"
and post WW II lending practices that led
to segregated suburbs in the first place
but don't give up
Baldwin says,
 "They are in effect, still trapped in a history
which they do not understand, and until they understand it,
they cannot be released from it…" but don't give up
Baldwin says,
"…bitterness is folly; it is necessary to hold on to the things
 that matter" AND "One must never, in one's own life,
accept these injustices as commonplace,
but must fight them with all one's strength.
This fight begins, however, begins in the heart
and it now has been laid to *my* charge
to keep my *own heart* free of hatred and despair,"
page 236, "Notes of a Native Son."

So we read, study, know and ask questions
about Black Wall Street of Tulsa Oklahoma
about Rosewood, Florida,
the Scottsboro Boys, Emmett Till, Medgar Evers, Cointel Pro,
the Central Park Jogger Defendants, learn 'bout Ida B. Wells,
Harriet Tubman, Madam CJ Walker, Marcus Garvey, Pedro Albisu
    Campos,
Ella Baker, Fannie Lou Hamer, Malcolm X, and Shirley
    Chisholm.
This is what it means to be an American...it's not a gun
it's a book, an essay, it's a pen
it's all about our education:
Martin Luther King, Jr, Stokely Carmichael, Josephine Baker,
    Huey Newton, Bobby Seale, Angela Davis, Bobby Hutton,
    Audrey Lorde, Cornel West, Ruth Ellis, Toni Morrison,
Ruth Gilmore. Herbert Aptheker, Michelle Alexander, and
    Déborah Berman-Santana.
This is what it means to be an American.....it's not a gun
it's a book, an essay, a poem, it's a pen
it's all about our education
it's all about the air and sunlight
to "keep our hearts free of hatred and despair"
as we tell the truth "to keep our hearts free"
bless you Jimmy,
as we tell the truth "to keep our hearts free"
bless you Jimmy.

Ode to Milton

We were not always like this
sitting still

We once threw spears
Ran blindly through angry streets
Loved the only beautiful carelessly

the past was a black box
for emergencies like time.

Use your arrogantly strong legs
Bring over that box
Cover your eyes against the glare

The Fates grope in the harsh light
Their lyrics deafen and distract
Do you know this tune?
It is the sound of regret.

October Robbers

October robbers razed my
womb, bled it black;
stole the fallen
leaves, and, with surgical precision,
pinned them onto branches,
rolling back the snow

They held the sun for ransom,
ate satsumas in the dark

October robbers crashed
through manholes;
aroused a lounging feline.
Amidst fallen stars,
she found a ragged world
on the floor.

October sheriff saw
nothing but a rock
among broken glass,
never saw exquisite angels
ground to dust along the floorboards

Autumn sister cut through gristle,
sizzled fat upon the stove,
sweetened sauerkraut with
wine, applesauce, and mustard

October thieves stole time,
swallowed up November
Brother scoured maples,
gathered scarlet hours,
reglazed forgotten tempos—

Hatchets hide in closets,
waiting for December.

The Ash Tree

He said he loved me
like doves nesting in our ash tree
and listened to my sorrow,
brought bouquets of water-colored
peonies and plumerias, red and pink.
In his arms I faltered while I swirled in fantasies
of tangos across the sky in slippers made of stars.

Those summer days we floated
on autumn leaves undressing
to reveal my hollow heart tangled in barbwire.
I said, "Forever,"
though the crows cawed a ragged song
about the never-ending spin
of infatuation's door.

He adored me like a silky dress flowing over me
while I drifted in the ballroom of masked monogamy.
I rode a raft of raven feathers on waves of mystery
that crashed the rocky shores of deception.
In the brittle night, I climbed the leafless ash.
My slippery grasp released his hand
The black moon rose, the sky went dead.

In dim-lit alleys, I scored sugared-love from dealers
who gnawed like desperate rats on infidelity's rot.
They wore fedoras on their brows
and offered rides for free.
Little did I know the cost as I watched my beloved suffer
in a storm of pain as he ran for cover
underneath the ash tree that had no leaves for shelter.

From behind the barren tree,
I came home, a blue jay, emptied of treachery,
a songbird that had learned to cry, a traitor that had no disguise.
Naked of my siren songs, I stumbled to his opened heart
revealed the track marks on my arms
from shooting romance cut with lies
to ease my tortured soul.

Dawn untied her rainbow hair and kissed the weeping rosebuds
below a canopy of lavender and orchids.
Spring bloomed white gardenias
like perfume intertwining with love's rising phoenix—
as we strung beads around our hearts,
made daisy chains connecting stars,
and read each other Rumi's poems beneath our blooming tree.

Culls

March leaves unfurl,
blossoms flower
playing host to bees.
Buds form, growing
into fleshy orbs,
while last season's culls
still hang in shadow
of more worthy fruit.

October leaves turn,
dropping in November.
Culls remain,
not big enough to keep
not juicy enough for pies,
applesauce,
a brown-bag lunch.

Tiny shriveled apples
no one wanted—
not even the worms—
cling to wire-thin twigs
through blowing winds,
freezing nights,
another season,
too stubborn to let go.

The Picture Taker

First, she thought about the shots she would take;
there was the available light to consider,
the right setting
and props to choose
perhaps
under the acacia tree
with a plain chair
turned backward
on which her child could lean, arms crossed.

She took her time
adjusting camera on tripod,
changing film speed,
measuring exposure,
all the while murmuring soft words
to relax her restless subject,
making a game of it.

Posing him to best advantage,
she tilted his chin,
arranged a lock of hair,
suggested he pretend to be mad
—or sad
to create a mood.

With lips slightly parted,
his sweet gaze
would forever burn in her eyes.
Like a believer in primitive magic,
she wondered if her camera
captured his soul.

Shades of White and Gray

Of all the photos depicting the fire,
red flames advancing
over fields of golden grass

against the blue-black night sky,
the most stark
was one in shades of white and gray.

Silent testimony to horror
were bleached bones of cattle
lying in ash,
rib cages prominent
like curved willow branches
too big for a helicopter ride,
overcome by heat, smoke,
hopelessness.

Found close together,
I wonder, if, in that last moment,
unlike humans and wild animals
racing down Atlas Peak,
they abandoned the idea of running and
simply sought comfort in one another.

Morning Walk

The man and his dog with matching limps
venture out each morning.
The man has a cane.
The dog does not.
They move in fits and starts,
stopping often, the dog to lift his leg,
the man to catch his breath.
They are like couples
who have grown old together,
adopting each other's mannerisms,
finishing each other's sentences.
Theirs is the perfect union,
an inspiration to those of us
who remain imperfect.

Solitude

Our life no longer
a *duet:* a *silo,*
rather, *toils due* to the
god of Fate Chosen.
My *soul tied* to this table
across from you, set in
solid silence. Sing!
My *loudest I* wants
her voice heard. You
duel it so you can
erase the lines
that *lied to us.* What
comes *due I lost.*
My shadow lives in
an *old suite* of stone.
Take these words to
dilute so you can undo
the *old tie* once
gentle between *us.*
Leave me the residue:
solitude

Mulled Blues

the great blue
standing alone
unreachable
wings open slowly
unsteady on the ground

Vermeer mulled two blues
one for the heron
the other for the sky
into which she flew
her milieu now

Unsteady Beauty

grief
standing alone,
untenable;
bound in this tight poem
unsteady beauty

do you know
how much I love you
she asked over and over,
do you remember the time
the time when

use both hands
grief in one
beauty in the other
place both on her heart
breathe

Haiku Journal

Cambodia

Angkor Hotel

> Whirlwind of purple,
> swirling maelstrom blocks my view.
> Bougainvillea!

River Cruise

> We pass floating
> houses. River-washed shirts hang:
> Silver, Black–Raiders!

Bayon Wat (part of Angkor Wat)

> Drawn to the temple,
> I pause. The ancient nun sits,
> smiles. First offering.

Thailand

Elephant Camp

Trust.

> Under the tent, the
> elephant's trunk massages
> the prone mahout's back.

Ride.

> On wrinkled skin
> we move across the river
> into the jungle.

Riverbank.

> The kingfisher sits
> on the slanting bamboo branch
> promising turquoise.

Temple Dogs

> Belonging to all,
> belonging to none, twenty-seven dogs
> fulfill Buddha's law.

River Kwai War Memorial, Misted Mountains

> Inside, remnants of war,
> sickness, death.
> Outside, serenity.

Bus Ride, Buddha's Way

> The bus jolts, stops. Snake
> on the road! We wait, watching
> it move to safety.

Wat Chantaram

> Millions of mirrors
> flash images of Buddha
> In silver slivers.

Alms Giving, Chiang Mai

> Pre-dawn. The monks
> eyes cast downward,
> wend their way down the mountain

> We offer our gifts:
> trays of rice, curry, fruit.
> A lotus flower.

We fill their alms bowls,
smile, bow. Kneel for
their chanted blessing.

Releasing the Birds

Nine finches flutter
in bamboo cage. Ninety baht:
Fly free, little birds!

Things I will never do in this lifetime

I'll never live in an adobe house in New Mexico,
walls two feet thick, recesses built into unexpected surfaces,
Navaho rugs on the floors, walls, sculptures in red clay,
an O'Keefe hanging in the bedroom,
ochre and umber washes coloring the kitchen,
redolent with hanging red chilis, purple garlic, onions...

I'll never live by the ocean in a redwood house,
angles slanting toward the sea, inside glass and stone
and the crash of waves predictable as the moon, punctuating
the pattern of my days ...

I'll never live in the house of the artist I'll never be,
a memory wherever my eyes alight, color cascading
in fabrics from Morocco, Turkey, Afghanistan, paintings
bold and vibrant, sculptures of women standing, sitting, encircling
     space,
randomness overlaid by a deep sense of structure ...

I'll never know the source of my draw to Egypt,
studying the ancient texts, knowing the feel of the earth
when the waters of the Nile recede.

I'll never know the origin of certain memories—
the cloistered life in Normandy,
tending sheep on the hills in Spain,
trekking with my wolfdogs in the frozen tundra,
painting frescoes in the caves of Cappadocia,
waking in the white hot buildings of ancient Greece,
vestal virgin to Helios, slave to priests, holding the
great sacrificial birds.

I'll never conduct a Mahler symphony or sing the role of Mimi
in Boheme, never again read Wallace Stevens all the way through
sitting on a small bed in Vermont, never read Finnegan's Wake...

I'll never spend an entire day in complete silence,
unencumbered by the need for food, for print, for voice.
I'll never live in perfect simplicity:
one table, one vase, one chrysanthemum,
one book of haiku.

A Branch of Tomorrow

the poet writes
as a branch of tomorrow
from the redwood tree
drops
into the room

We see this green branch
fall gently across the grain
the wood not long ago
part of another tree, the table
top sanded and polished
sides with jagged memory

but the green branch of tomorrow
almost in our hands
changes everything
The poet says,
We are close
enough to childhood,
so easily purged
of whatever we thought we were to be

we thought
we knew where we stood
gathered there
in the room
around this table where
our stories have been
twice told

we see the dream of our childhood
filled with remembrances of earlier lives
forgotten as we grew but now
remembering
the sun-god's white-domed temple
the endless sands
of the Bedouin desert
and we feel the pull of Demeter
who shadowed us
through these many lives

the edge of our belief is just beyond
this life we are living with dreaming eyes
we gather up our stories
rich with sighthounds and white ravens
knowing
the branch of tomorrow
is built on today
lying ready
the poet says
to bud forth

\

Note: italicized words from Robert Duncan's "Food for Fire,
Food for Thought"

Stay with Me

Leaning on our secret gate to the stars
we mused on the mysteries of the universe,
the mind
the soul
of love
inside the tangled folds of our loving coverlet.
We recited passionate poems solemnly

Months after you left
your scent is still
on my chest my loins
my lips,
and the air stands back refusing to take your place
when I reach for your body
that is no longer there
next to mine.
My heart breaks
again.

I drove three thousand miles from you,
with the splintered echo of your spite
ringing bitter in my ear,
your voice pouncing from the blacktop
at every twist and turn in the road.

But sometimes you still walk in my room
where you have never set foot
as sure of your hold over me as
Dante's Francesca's hold on a silent Paolo.
Your dusty voice murmurs
nothing sweet in my ears,

your words tinged with spite
a trinity of despair bitter
as a stone in the heart of a peach.

On lonely nights too often to deny
your lover's voice tinkles
in my bedroom like ice in a glass.
Your amber skin shines in my memory
in the silver moon light.

And at these times — I forget and cast out
bitter memories
of being blown about
in your whirling storm,
and whisper,

"Stay with me
a little while
until I sleep.
Just stay with me until I sleep."
As my tear-stained face
shines in the glow
of the amber night-light
without you.

Patrice Deems

Race of the Dragonflies

I watch you circle
The wind's
speedway
Golden wings
reflecting sun,
and imagine
an engine
humming cherubic tunes
from inside
your jeweled fuselage

Fly closer
tiny dragons

Two of you came to visit
our ocean balcony last night
You lay so still
We tried to save you,
gently sliding a paper stretcher
underneath
Placed you on the rail
Hoped you would catch your breath
and fly off

More and more of you
frantically
pattern the sky
Taking off
from Sea Grape and Palm trees
Flying jewelry
Magnificent woven wings
propelling turquoise pendants

Six months to live
You swarm, frenzied
making infinity loops
death spirals

As nymphs
you spent years
escaping predators,
floating in marshy water—
When you emerge and metamorphose,
you are still scared,
sometimes— to death

Sadly,
one morning
We found your fairy squadron
at-the-ready,
in formation
Vanquished
In one
Autumn night

Egret

leggy egret
struts the shore
elegant white beachcomber
perusing its kingdom
mired in zen
never stresses about
how to get through the day
doesn't know butterflies exist
blind to all
except food, enemies, mating possibilities
slowly turns head
left to right
no chiropractics necessary

Every Minute

Every minute, as precious as a gold coin, presses
the mountain forward — time to move, get ready, now!

Night falls to the tick tock, tick tock. Coyotes.
To hear them some nights, brings in the lunar cold.

Over lunch, jicama and cabbage, she tells us her news—
marriage on the rocks. And, here, take some Meyer lemons.

The rim of sun glimmery, then snuffed, the mottled reds.
After Qi Gong, we compare sightings of the supermoon,

.

When do stars fade into dawn's pale? Blankets and comfort
of the husband's snores, nine hours ahead, in Kuwait, though.

Mountain Air

The cold air at night seeps in
through the open window
opened wide for the cool

Stars and dreams slip in—
the baby takes her first step
a loud snore lands you on the moon

Or is it China where you find
yourself robed in red silks
breathing sage incense

The once azure skies milkened
now soft cover for sleep
and the wild goji berries

intimacy in black and white

after buzzing
and circling about
it landed on my neck

I did not whisk it away

instead
was taken back in time
to a photography class

there   we talked about an image

a woman lay naked in the mid-day sun
grains of sand and beads of sweat
accented the contours of her body

she was still

a fly had settled
below her belly
its mouth touched her skin

she had not whisked it away

translucent wings
like bare skin
glistened in the sun

caught in the moment

the black and white image
radiated the heat of two bodies
captured on film

a still life fixed in time

At 3 A.M.

The world is quiet
The sun is asleep
Stars yawn

Stillness ...
Silence ...

Rivers rush
Earth quakes
Volcanoes spew
Tornadoes roar
Hurricanes lash
Drought cracks

The Earth ... not silent
The Earth ... not asleep

We are silent
We are not awake

Brennan, gone too soon...

(for his mother Sheila)

He roared like a lion
like the ocean
crashing against the rocky shore
(insides thrashing one struggle to the next).

They say still waters run deep.
Sometimes noisy waters run deeper.
Run and jump and probe
trying to find purchase,
or
trying to find quiet.

There's a hole in the bottom of the deep-blue sea.
The blue-green sea that is the color of his eyes.
Always bringing him home.
Bringing him to his mother's door.
Bringing him to his mother's shore.

He's there in the laugh of the seagulls.
In the storms that rumble and tumble your head
only to bring sun the next morning.
He's in the clouds that darken your door one minute
only to break into amusing fluffy shapes the next.

He'll turn up and surprise you
just when you're least expecting it.
He was, and always will be, after all.

Robin Gabbert

Terri

She is not particularly pretty
and her nose is a little too strong,
but as the heat and light of an oven
changes a little of this and a little of that
into a delicious dessert
she smiles.

Bar Crawl

A bar crawl it was
Been a long time
My girl was with me
So I knew I would be fine
At one place, we ate
Low and behold
We ended up at a birthday
For a twenty-five-year old
A lift operator and mechanic
Is what he told us he did
As his friends slammed shots
I almost envied the kid
At some point therein
I took him aside
I pointed to my chest
And said hey twenty-five
Being young is really nice
Because there's nothing you fear
But look at me at sixty-five
Your job is to get here
Remember me when you do
Cause I'll be long gone
Your journey won't be easy
Lots will go wrong
I'm living till one hundred
He said with a grin
I replied goals are important
And that's a good place to begin
But to get there, you know
You have to get here
As I pointed to my chest

And I tried to be clear
Then I ended the lesson
Sipped some more beer
And I wondered if he listened
Yet alone if he could hear
Then he slammed his tequila
Sucked on a lime
And we melted into the evening
We had a good time.

Death in Hawaii

for Chris

We heal then weep
Or weep then heal
We rally for each other
Filling the hole we feel
Or try to fill
With busyness each day
Wondering if or when
This sadness will go away
It's not unique
This feeling we feel
It circles the world
And it makes life real
Time heals everything
Our mom used to say
But I wish it was faster
Then it seems today
As a new sunrise
Wakes up the world
Out on the lanai
Just me and my girl.

Nature of Things

We had just finished singing
Happy birthday to my dad
Tears welled up in his eyes
I don't think from being sad
Both my sisters, and I
Could see from where we were
Emotion was on display
My little sister could not stop hers
I made a comment to my mom
My sister had mascara tracks
"Yeah, I know" my mother said
She worries about your dad
She wants us to live forever
And you know, we just can't"
And there's the rub, don't you know
That limited time we're here
Time seems long when we're young
And short after living many years
I too, want them to live forever
Or at least until I'm gone
But that's just not the nature of things
As our lives still move along
Forget holding back the tide
It is not death I fear
But moving through life with purpose
Has become abundantly clear

October Remnants

Oh how I've missed
These smoke-filled skies
And that burning sensation
I feel in my eyes
The orange sunsets
And the pretty sunrise
As I breathe in the remnants
Of other people's lives

Reconciliation

Descendent of Aboriginal Warriors
Dots and swirls
Inked into his flesh
His ancestral traditions are honored

Warrior fists and feet pound
The rhythm of welcome
To white-collared men
And high-heeled women

Rich brown skin pales
Under florescent lights
Bare feet pivot on
Industrial carpeting

Outdoors his starry maps are
Obscured by street lights
Bird songs once known are dust
Their wisdom entombed in pavement

Descendent of Aboriginal Warriors
His palm itches for the weapon
That would send all the others
Back to their own shores

Memorial day

I lie throughout the world,
Like random fallen leaves.
An ancient glacial relic
Swaying with sea things in rusted hulks.
Drifting with wind and sand.
Impaled upon nameless coral where the sea now
laps the beach in aquamarine.

My world was fire and thunder
darkness, rain, fear, and
numbness in my toes.
A world of mud, freezing mud,
stinking jungle mud, blood and urine mud.
No sun that didn't sear, wind that didn't tear.
No night with stars and dreams.

No bugle call with flag unfurled, or young girls laughing.
Or academic pondering of universal meaning.
No love or peace.
My world was dull pain, sharp pain,
sunburned eyes, smoke, stench.
Death without mourning.
Life without hope, without God, without glory.

I can't go home because
I have no name.
I am a voice from nowhere
whispering
"I have lost you.
Have you forgotten me?"

A Summer Parade

On my summer's walk I see:
Luminous lilac chicory wink through tall, dry grasses
Blue and white agapanthus rocket into bloom, everywhere
Girls, small and smaller, on bikes, head geared, waiting for mom
A cluster of padlocks cling to the schoolyard fence, coding
    anything, nothing

Tiny yellow daisies spark the lawns
Lone crow stamps the grass nosing for worms
Another, half a football field away, as the crow flies
Robust robins checker the soccer field worming
In another field flocks of crows and gulls standoff beak to beak

Yapping dogs dog-parking
A mother power runs, pushing her twins ahead of her, fresh as
    summer
Preschoolers and mothers fill the swings, the jungle gym, the
    slider, with screams and laughter
People walk dogs, dogs walk people

In swirls of pond algae tiny tadpoles squirm
Red-winged blackbirds rustle the reeds
Proud Canada geese parade across the path
Swimming baby ducks in a row follow mom

Clouds of golden algae clog the stream
Golden lichen gilds the oak tree trunk
Bright red geraniums in pots welcome me
At my door

Balancing Act on Benton Street

Nothing on the high wires
outside my window
this morning—
no racing squirrels
or spangled walkers
putting one foot in front
of the next,
toe-heel, toe-heel,
arms parallel to the wire
holding onto bamboo,
a crowd hushed below
awaiting a sacrifice.

I am alone,
imagining balances
and descents,
the relief of falling
into sheer space,
of letting go
of everything—
and the sun isn't
even out yet.

Dimly Lit Cafe on San Stefano

Wrapt by muzzy solitude and ghosts
I can't walk away the blues today.
I'm homesick, that's all. But this café—
round tables, small chairs, striped awning—
here are friends and wine from Melnik.
Amidst talk of Derrida and words, we see
the night fold in like a black down quilt
figured with small white stitches.

Displaced

Words have left me
dispossessed
I close my mouth silently weep
they are wandering loose
scattered like will-o-wisps among stars
skittering before me like oak leaves in wicked autumn wind
I catch one or two
they make no sense
I nail them to paper
waiting for the voice to speak
waiting for my universe to wake me up
whisper in my ear as I fall asleep

thoughts drift off like smoke from my cigarette
I try to inhale them   but they're gone
they do not play as they used to
running rampant
unschooled in behavior
I love them best of all then
exuberant rowdy beasts

they've become bits of static sound
crackling crumbs

I need to take them to the ocean
the river
sit in silence
wait for that sideways look
when they are ready to divulge

I've been collecting stones
instead of words a substitute for emotion within
the stones are keeping me here
that will do for now

Caged

We collect scraps
stones bones
rain-soaked sticks shards
speaking to us
I will inspire you
I have something to say
listen

we snuggle them close
mine
place in a bowl
set on a shelf
barely look at again
we forget to talk
to wait
to listen

our patience gathers dust while we seek anew

we think to release them to native lands
still do not let them go
trapping them
as surely as we
imprison ourselves
in the wild
we felt their essence
captive
they swallow their soul
remain silent

untamed, unbroken together
we made sense

walls oh walls
we barely breathe
unnatural sounds surround
hearts and ears close against
frenzied spirit
freedom we long for
while it batters at the door

Staying Put

settle down, restless feet
there comes a time
when you no longer
need to see it all

time to let things settle—
drop to the earth
put down roots
notice mysteries
of the neighborhood:
symphony of birdsong
children laughing down the street
sweet pink blooms on waking trees

you're not settling for less
to skip plane tickets,
foreign trips, new cars
simply accept what surrounds you
embrace all things
in your own sparkling universe

so it's settled:
we'll live to the fullest
right here
in our own backyard

Tangerine

your cousin the orange
is difficult to breach
all autumn-colored skin
stuck to fruit so close
it defies peeling
wants to be squeezed tight

you, precious tangerine,
live loose in your crinkly coat
small but proud
yield your juices
most generously
to my prying fingers—
sweet

Dew

dew drips from green leaves
like undeserved tears
mere moist remains of
morning fog
young day yearns
for sunshine
while I remember your voice
which hasn't warmed me
for a long, long time

A Loss that Every Other Loss Fits Inside

(For Laura)

The kid on the line
to order ice cream -
I would avoid talking
to her except that
she reminded me
of you
her tattoos piercings short haircut
and so
I asked her "do you recommend
a flavor?" yes she knew them all,
used to work here,
was glad to share
her knowledge.
her unexpected warmth
swept over me
a bridge
to a world
unknown before
and once suspect.

And every tattooed arm and
every short haired girl
and every soft cat curled
against the most comfortable chair
reminds me of you
and your absence, as loud
as the buzzing of my phone
ready to receive your signal.

Sometimes the book falls off the shelf.

Sometimes the winds whip up the flags
on my path. For a moment I expect you.
There is no time I don't remember you.

So Pilgrims bring their offerings and ancient gifts
hold potions no one can decipher.

Oh won't you follow the Poet's lyre
and find your way back here!

Perhaps the little one who calls to me
delighted and unfettered
by emotions
too complicated to unravel
will heal this injury of unrequited love
I have for you my lost and wounded child.

From the poem "What It Sounds Like" by Forrest Gander

Daughter My Daughter

born with the cord
wrapped round your neck —
tied to me
so I wouldn't ever let you go.

Last night you labored
to give birth and I
breathed with you
feeling the push of life,
walking about my house
on the razor's edge of time
while you worked so hard
to bring forth
a new being.

How strong this cord
that tugs through me,
tying one life to another

like those Russian dolls,
one contained in the next,
a new generation pulls us
into another dimension.

At this precise moment
we are more than
our small differences.
we are linked
like the shelter in our garden
built without nails,
ancient wooden boards, notched

one to the next.
we form a great web.
a molecular matrix,
a temple
to life.

For Fran

(a tribute)

My teacher you
bring out the poetry in me
you smile at my foibles
and glance toward me with love.
Like a doctor
you extract
what's built up
under the skin.
All these words
accumulated
from years of picking at the scabs,
neglecting
to clean old wounds.
Like a surgeon
you remove the unnecessary -
no need to summarize
or explain.

I arise an awkward bird from my cluttered nest
and tilt my wings on the warm air currents
created by your reassuring smile.

The cream
rises to the top,
the honey
is pulled from the blossom
by your kind and careful words.
I notice now
the scent of sprouted white narcissus
on the driveway.
And I respond
without apology
with a poem.

Mara Lynn Johnstone

Where Do You Get Your Ideas?

Here, read this article.
You'll love it.

What's it—
"Manhole Cover Launched Into Space"?

Yes! There were nuclear bombs, you see,
and tests for them,
and a deep hole,
with a metal cover...

Wow, it's going to travel forever.
Unless it hits something.

Yeah—

DIBS I'm writing it!
Alien society
It wrecked something
Now they're mad
Where is my pen??

Tough Choice

Any power, you say?
Oh, there are some good ones.
Flying is one of the greats.
Stopping time would be endlessly useful.
Shapeshifting would be fun, and it would also let me fly,
    so two points there.
But I think the best choice—

"Mommy?"

Never mind. New plan.
The super power to make children sleep.
You laugh—
I could change the world.

Small Magics

The multivitamins come in three colors,
and which one comes out of the bottle first
dictates how good the day will be

The bottle of mouthwash
should face label-side out
for the best toothbrushing experience

The fork chosen from the drawer
should be one with long tines,
or the meal will be tainted

The items on the desk
should be arranged
just so
for an ideal writing environment

And maybe it's because I am a writer,
in the habit of Noticing Things,
that I see all these small magics
for what they are.

Cornobble

There is something elegant
and eloquent
and delightfully, gloriously crude
about slapping someone with a fish

There is simply no comparison

Nothing can match the flop
and the smell
and the indignity of it all

It is with this in mind
that I have procured a rubber fish

For I have several friends writing a novel this month
and if they need encouragement
to meet their word count,
I will be ready.

Slow Drift of an Untethered Mind on a Sunny Afternoon

A thought appears
A sudden memory
Some shooting star
Extinguishing all others

A memory
Its randomness
Extinguishing all others
Your face in profile

Its randomness
That small telling gesture
Your face
As I knew you

That small telling gesture
Unconscious in its revelations
Yes I knew you
Something passed between us

In its revelations
Something was understood, settled
Passed between us
Though really nothing happened

Something was settled
As if nothing happened
And really nothing happened
But what was that

As if nothing
Some shooting thought
But what is that
A star appears

Briahn Kelly-Brennan

All Along the Serious Day

Moods moving like clouds
or wanderings of the unplanted
Sun floats in its shell of sky
five naked ladies
turn pink at the sight
despite the urgent explanation of the leaves

When four frogs under an upturned bucket sing "La Donna E
 Mobile"
a rabbit in a black leather jacket will enter your dreams
and we will drink a book a day
as sylvan sounds
rub the bowl of your ear
until it rings
until it sings
until it opens

I Find Myself

I find myself laughing
Voices from the picnic
Mimic a chorus of crickets
Afternoons always sound so warm

Voices from some picnic
Waves of leaves rustle a breeze
The warm sounds of afternoon
In the slow light of a low hanging sun

Leaves rustle the breeze
A mirage of flat-footed frogs
In the slow hanging light
I start to slip under its wake

Flat-footed frogs mirror
A picnic of mimicking crickets
I wake with a start
To find myself laughing

Sister

She's reading
Focused as a frog on a fly
Brilliant as the beginning of time
Willing to enter another's moment

Solid like the North Pole
She bends light and beads the years
Stopping to illuminate
the one molecule that matters

The Wind

Gales and gusts
do sailors trust
to carry one
safely across
the Sea.

Billows blasting,
blazing bright.
Fiery furnace,
blood red
the Night.

Matchstick timbers,
Dante's Wake.
Thank God,
and others
who saved so many
from
ill Fate.

Tent flaps flapping,
lashing loud,
like a Serpent,
tongue hissing,
lightning licking,
High,
Dark Clouds.

Wind whips and cracks,
oak branches snap.
Thunder rumbles, mumbles
Beyond the ridge.

A gulp,
I swallow,
a sigh,
I Breathe.

Sudden. Still.
A gentle whisper,
Near.

"You need not worry
nor tremble,
in Fear.

No cause or reason
for Concern

It's just the Wind, child—
And,
there are
no trees left
to Burn."

Just Enough to See

On touring "Monet, the Later Years" at the
de Young Museum, San Francisco

I confess I never liked
Monet's bridge, the
Japanese tea bridge he
painted so often
arching like an interruption
over his exquisite water lilies

But it is always good
to see something anew
to be delightfully surprised
especially when you
are over seventy and
think you know everything
about yourself

It was his painting of the
bridge in bright reds
deep browns and greens
that did it
dabbed and slashed
across the canvas
like a storm

The bridge invisible
except for the mere
hint of an arch
just enough to imagine it
just enough to long for it

As Monet must have done
cataracts closing in
head still on fire
ushering in a new way
of seeing

Safe

I wanted to write about Amal
the Yemeni girl dying of starvation
her portrait published
in the New York Times
five days before she died

I wanted to write about how
she had no muscle, no fat
just bone
skin draped over bone
over ribcage
protruding
like ripples in a pond

I wanted to write about
how her face
was serene
turned to the side
sparing me accusation

I wanted to write about how my
heart caved in on itself anyway
how my legs went weak
my body limp
as I saw all of humanity
go over the cliff

I wanted desperately to capture all this
at the very smallest least
bear witness to her suffering

But when I started to write
a different poem came out
a poem about the time
I was camping in Montana
how I was up before daybreak
wrapped in a blanket
waiting for the sun to emerge
over the mountains

How I saw a doe pass in front of me
stepping deliberately towards
the river bottoms
how she came back with her fawn
hidden all night in the willows
licked clean of scent

How they headed up the
hillside together
disappearing into the spruces
to forage

How that memory shelters me
the doe always coming
the fawn always safe

The Invitation

Canyon de Chelly National Monument
Chinle, Arizona

I could have easily missed it
not wandered down to the far end
or turned my gaze away
at the crucial moment

Worse,
I could have seen it
dismissed it
too unlikely, too otherworldly

But that's not what happened

It was early spring
we had the place inexplicably
to ourselves
Spider Rock jutting up
from the valley floor
brilliant red sandstone
against clear blue sky

I imagined Spider Woman
atop the rock
weaving her sacred web of connections
while streams cut the canyon
and the Dineh walked into the world

It was further along
deeper into the canyon
that I noticed the ravens

two of them, flying along the rim
tossing something between them
catching it in their beaks
tossing it back one to the other

I stood still, mesmerized
the precision required
to account for the wind
their movement
racing through my mind

The ravens passed closer
with each new toss
closer to the canyon wall
closer to me

Then the juniper sprig
no heavier than a feather
landed at my feet

Raven catching my eye
as it made the toss

The Weekend News

The Arctic is burning
Sao Paulo dark with smoke
Icelanders mourn a beloved glacier
world leaders struggle with the
consequences of "unprecedented"

I try to shake off the ache of it
go outside to watch morning light
when a tiny pearl appears
at eye level beside me
suspended in mid air

I blink, look closer
a spider comes into focus
dangling from a strand of silk
the sun catching it just so
turning its flesh-colored body
opalescent white

I stand watching
as the spider
so small in this big world
continues downward
head first
toward solid ground

Pale Morning Dun

Observe the mayfly
Ephemerella
pale morning dun
crawling out of her body
emerging from the water
to a beautiful spring day

She rests in alder shrubs
hardening her wings
producing her eggs
waiting
for the ancient call
to join the swarm
to mate

She flies low over the water
depositing an egg delicately
here and there and there
until she is spent
a lifetime in three days

Is it sad
such beauty, so brief
or profound

What is time but relative
human life a heartbeat
compared to a redwood
compared to a rock

To My Ancestors

To you, whom I did not know.
To you, who took the steps
to create your future
to carve a new path as your world
turned upside down.

To you, who left your country,
your soil,
to brave the seas
and take a chance on life—
to start over
to have hope
to linger in thoughts and dreams and aspirations.

To you, who created the footsteps
to continue life
to want more
to nurture and bring forth a new generation.

To you, who let me be born
out of the desire of the human soul,

I thank you.

Beneath the Surface

Beneath the surface
a firefighter reflects,
even cries.
They did it — they didn't let the fire
spread beyond 101.
They were not going to repeat
what happened two years ago.
They were not going to
let this one kill more people and
burn thousands of homes.
Beneath the surface
even though 77,000 acres burned,
they succeeded.

Beneath the surface
the new CEO of PG&E gets a
2.5 million dollar salary.
What if *that* money
went to update equipment, poles,
put wires underground?

Beneath the surface we pay our
electric bill by flashlight.

Beneath the surface
no matter how many households
had their electricity shut off,
a single jumper on a tower broke
and set off a spark
that seems to have started it all.

Beneath the surface
I'm exhausted from carrying around
all my valuables in and out of my car
for four days.
Bad air still hurts my lungs,
I had to cancel my class and now
I'm in bed with a cold.
I blew a fuse last night.
Did they turn our power off again?
No, I still see light in the next room,
but how that thought sent panic
through my body.

Above the surface
we'll get past this one.
Friends will help friends
and life will go on.

But beneath the surface
we are living powerless to the wind,
in fear of flames
and always knowing what we will pack
the next time around.

Thirst

They are all older than me —
the mountains, seas, trees.
They hold the wisdom of the years,
the secrets to survive.
They know not to fret
over small things,
that the world goes on around them
crazy and blind.
They remain steadfast in presence,
all drinking from the same pool —
the one at the center of the universe,
the one offering me a sip.

Passion's Bright Fire

Like clay waiting to be shaped,
I can become what you want,
with your hand there to guide me.
If I don't break.

Tears of joy and sadness, can
soften clay for loving hands
passion determines the form
Love brings it to life

The potter's wheel is done
Light the kiln and stoke the coals
but take care, lest passion's bright
fire destroy the pot.

So Much Forgotten

The look, a veiled glance, a word
The jokes, clever talk, secrets
Marriage on the knife's edge
so much forgotten

Passion fuels betrayal
Naked bodies crushed together
Entrapped by the scent of sex
A lifetime destroyed

Reverie

He entered the sanctuary in the half-sleep
of this morning's silence,
but trellises of time and talk
had separated him from that first moment.
He tried now to step back, to step across.

Each morning has its particular texture of silence.
He sought out the most familiar elements.
Silence can be like a cat's paws
navigating the warm bodies beneath bed covers.
Silence nestles in the sunlit cheek
or alights on a petal of bare shoulder.
It catches even in the skrakking of
homely birds hidden in eucalyptus trees.
Maybe it's not the stimuli themselves
that are silent,
but the tender places they evoke
in the forest of his brain.

Inside the hall,
he gazes at the muted faces of his companions—
each wrapped in its own tapestry of silence.
One takes notes, without a pen;
another bends her head
softly, as if under the weight of one moth.
A third, eyes closed, may be trying
to recover a dream he wished he'd almost had.

His own dream had been of a farmish-field,
strewn with its fretwork of debris. He had
somehow to cross it, easing into a waist-deep ditch—
to pee, or perhaps to swim? And
when he returned, it was to tug
the wrinkled sheet over his features
like an incoming wave, a curtain—
long, slow, certain.

Mark Meierding

Floating/Amorphia

In pond or pool or vat, you know
that water yields your body buoyant, yes,
but won't it also weight you down?
Water enfolds your unison of flesh,
like yolk within its albumen,
so that your arms sweep forth
as if in sable sleeves,
and fingers feel thick and mute
as winter mittens. Water's mum motion
wants to swallow you every second
or flop you over dead-down whale.
When finally climbing up and out,
you're grateful for the ladder's singular rungs.

Mightn't soaking be a healthy enterprise
for astronauts? Let water's firm resistance
counteract their cosmic loss of body mass?
Imagine, in his interplanetary urn: the spaceman,
veggie smoothie at his hand's command
and naked forearms to confirm
the borders of his hot tub's brim.

But wait. In space there is no gravity.
Those gallons would arise as globule jellies
that when he tries to grasp them,
rupture into dandelion fairies.
This vision makes my tummy queasy,
like airline stories of crashing passengers' entrails.

Art finds forms to limn our landscape
and to orient our posture's view,
the way white contrails intersect
the canvas of a pale blue sky.
Yet there's neither brush nor ink
to render the sinew of liquid
or skeleton of space.

Observations on Mortality

My dear particularity,
this fleeting molecule of me—
one atom want and three of fear—
shivers as the eons near.
To foresee what revels will grace the ship
after I've signed off the trip
feels like Christmas laid 'round the tree:
all for others, none for me.

They say that when you're plainly dead,
your name's erased, so that your soul
can merge into a Greater Whole.
Unhappily, I suspect instead
you're left behind. You add no fraction—
a loss no louder than subtraction
of a fragile shadow from the sea.
Indeed, to swell accordingly,
Ocean births *new* souls. Why re-brew
the residue of me and you?

Perhaps there is a Master Reason
a human only gets one season.
Yet I, I deem it most unkind,
this casual snuffing of *my* mind.

Traveler's Prayers

Polytheism

Almost sunset
on the shuttle bus.
Frozen forests
of bare branches
etched flatly through
frosted window screens.
Sun-dollar floats
in silver mesh
opposite the minted moon.
Bus turns.
    On this moment of a winter evening,
praise to the glittering moon
and several glassy suns.

Matins

Dawn on the airplane.
Just before take-off,
a head-turn away,
the clouds have grown rose,
grown roses in
profusion. Fuchsia rays
grace the inhabitants
on the left of the cabin.
Like their shadows,
I bow my head

Vernal Meditation en Route to Mountains

Grasses and trees flaunt fresh green.
Clouds shift their colors,
distend the bellows of their lungs.
In luxury, I ride by
in my carriage drawn by fossils.
Approaching Calaveras Big Trees State Park,
Pinyons, Ponderosas, Jeffries
are marked with orange tags or
their own orange needles.
66 million trees in the Sierra
dead of drought and bark beetle.

May my miles be worthy.
May my stories serve.
May my sharings, growings, deserve.

Living Mandala

At a Tshechu, annual sacred festival in
Domkhar. Bhutan

1.

Follow me to a small country
where trees in new yellow leaf
stand before black mountains,
where clouds curdle above,
with sun seeping through.
Where distant Himalayas look
like the exquisitely chipped rim
of the world's sugar bowl.
Sit with me and the local populace
in a monastic courtyard
while temple bells gong
and drums beat out
da-da-DUM-dum-dum.

2.

Watch while a dozen monks
in masks of the zodiac,
in yellow skirts with rainbow
petticoats, emerge from
the temple, their feet bare,
chests, too, but for richly
embroidered bibs and straps.
And on the grass and flagstones,
they dance, whirl and
twirl, lift feet, toss ribboned
crests, ears, horns, gin up winds
with the sticks they carry.

Rooster, ox, rat and all spin like clocks
and counter-clocks, the mandala
of their ring wheeling in a circle game.
The winds blow hot and cold.
The temple horns blow cool.
At last spent, each takes a solo exit,
helped up steps by other monks —
ones not drunk on dance.

3.

After the barest of intervals, the monk dancers
will be back in different masks
to again leave all on the flagstones.
They will repeat all day. Meanwhile
divine jesters will orchestrate with smirk

masks and phallus prods. They grin,
teach steps, poke people, invite themselves
onto audience laps. It's understood these
tricksters must stay inside the gates.

Cymbals are singing and the monks are
back in red brocade, whirling, holding
swords of purification, and spinning.
Have I ever witnessed someone
dancing themselves into a frenzy
for the enlightenment of my soul?
Yes

In Wilderness

a villanelle with lines from Handel's Messiah

Like sheep, we each turn to our own way,
deaf to each other and animal kin, and
that voice that's crying in the wilderness.

I find myself in a blur of snow
with bleakest blue along horizon's edge.
I'm astray and turned to my own way.

And then a distant form, a shambling shape,
and sounds like moans and hollering,
a voice that's crying in the wilderness.

The bear is white and shuffles up to me.
She touches her nose to mine, and kneels.
I wonder if she, too, has lost her way.

I climb her back, her bristles thick, well-greased.
Her back accepts me like a cub. I fit.
She lifts her voice again, and sings her woes.

Beneath her fur, I see her tough black skin.
Sure-footed with snowshoe paws, hairy toes,
she's suited to this place, is not astray.

We travel to the edge of crumbling ice where
four hundred miles to swim for food has made her lose
her cub. I hope I'm not so far astray I can't
make heard this wilderness so filled with cries.

Firefly Lantern

Mom would puncture holes
in the lids of Mason jars
for us to catch fireflies, caution
us to admire our lanterns for just
awhile, then set the fireflies free.

I was mesmerized by my lanterns
with their green and gold glimmerings;
when the lights dimmed, I'd remember
that my toy was filled with living things,
their lives dependent on me.

Sometimes, I'd forget to set them free,
find a jar on its side in the morning dew;
I can still see one firefly, nearly dead, yet
able to crawl out, clinging to a blade of grass,
its light useless against midsummer sun.

I look back across the years, across the field
to my childhood home, deepening twilight
revealing a darker sky than I recall. I see
one firefly, then a few more. When I was
a child, their numbers rivaled the stars.

Piccarda

— *Dante meets an acquaintance in Paradise: Piccarda,*
whose brother forced her to leave a convent for a
marriage that advanced her family's fortunes. Dante
wonders why this places her in the lowest circle of
Paradise, farthest from God. Beatrice suggests that
Piccarda could have refused to leave the convent.

i.

He's gone, the brother who stole me from my God,
deployed me in the hot and climbing world I loathed.
Gone, the grasping shape he made among the assets,
tall and narrow as the caliper, the insect.

I did not refuse, I wore obedience against his violence.
And fear. I did not love my God as some did, with heat
and nearness, with all the heedless colors
of the poppies tearing in His bright wind.

I did not even curse the different, curving view,
the black and singing circles of the birds
who entered the round and windy trees
and placed one rustling dark inside another.

I almost loved the distance, the apartness:
The music of longing
that grows slowly in a heart
where certain strings are silenced.

ii.

I knew myself as one of many soft shapes
touching the dark with pale hands,
a palm flat and upward like a blossom
staving off or ceding with a little, fragrant sigh.

A woman doing what was asked. Obedience
still around me like a skin of tilting stars.
And underfoot the many moods to be watched
like the little lizards who sometimes touched me.

Each loss of fervor and desire seemed
a dream only or a passing silty breeze,
a wind small and yellow, pleasing
like a line of dying, floating butterflies.

The diminishment inconsequential,
as I was.

iii.

Will you ask me:
How then did I grieve
the loss of my heated, vehement God,
His sorrow at the softness of my leaving?

Imagine a world with two bodies:
One made of the leaning of horses;
One made of the falling of sand.
Two thicknesses like islands on a map.

See the dream, the landscape
where the sand is moving,
slips through the dark like blood.
Breakage the color of glass. That is me.

iv.

And I sing the God who put me here:
I who set aside the rose-white veil,
tearing my vow—the vow I made
from an imagined cool and gentle place.

I see from distance into beauty here,
with eyes of mirror and water.
I wade in the color of moon,
the slowly turning, peaceful circle.

I sing the small song, fold in my eyes
the taller, wandering stars,
the glow that holds its white breath.

Caliban

i.

The forest puts a shimmer in its animals,
a binding root of light or sound or want.
A kind of green and tangled dreaming.

Then those other creatures came, the talking animals
who floated loudly out of the edge of the world
on the splotches of their books and grievances.

They could not find the wordless things,
black noises in the trees, all
that was caught or stilled or falling there—

It was I who mimed what hid from them,
the visitors as strange to me as birds,
bright in their ranks and coverings.

ii.

The forest mostly loves its creatures,
rolls them in light and dark and yellow
birds who live in a space that flickers.

It flies their colors in the tall of summer,
on the rattle of river. Colors that will sleep
when the forest smells moon or the white of winter.

I think the forest loves my eye, my silver eye
in its furry, weeping slot. Its veer and sway, the way
it shakes excitement out of empty air.

The way it knows the colors, the temporary gibber
of the light. That's the view I understand
and must call beautiful and true. Must love.

iii.

I gave them all I knew, so quickly, shuffling
as if dancing with the height I saw in their eyes,
the strange brightness of the air around them.

They took it all, then laughed and forgot me.
And I saw myself as if for the first time: ugly.
One of the creatures that spit and slide

Along the afterlight, a daub, a blot
that swims briefly when the lamp goes out.
A dark thing living in the light by sufferance.

Perhaps I held back something, some thought
that will fly me out of this blackness.
Some spell that will make them narrow and still.

That will make them scuttle in the light.
Make them crawl like fire on a wick
through the meaner dark they dream in.

For I have seen the blue-white cliff of who they are.
Let them roll back over the edge of the world.
Let them rattle there like a pile of scorpions.

Jupiter

The middle is where I am and how I see.
A place between two colors, two temperatures:
the red of Mars and Saturn's cold and silver mirror.

I sit in the chair of equal distance, waiting,
judging. There are children there
who love the patient helix of my ear.

I hear the little wind of their voices.
I am the tree that sucks the dark and exhales
a small white flower and a fragrance.

A boy touches the ancient green of a frog
and knows with his hot, smooth hand
the way the colors jump in the world.

Revisiting Hamlet

Who is it that has everything
and owns nothing,
lives without compromise,
dances on life's stage
without the light of knowledge
nor music of the ages?

Who is it that can find a path
without seeking help,
devours the present,
and cannot be sated?

Who is it comes to me at night,
wasting my sleep with past wrongs,
when acceptance is a shadow
never seen in darkness?

Sharing Mozart

we dance
to a Mozart concerto
in the concealment
of unlit candles
and clouds
of pungent smoke

eyes closed
breath heated
sharing
the aloneness
of movement

Color Yourself

Swirls going to where? Into and out of mind
A circle of imagination

Color dancing itself toward freedom
To the Zen of cerulean consciousness

Grasping at desire crushed into a million hues
All joys, despair, fear - we relish our limitless spirit

Into the deepest depths of maroon, until, with an aching sigh
We touch the sensuousness of yellow

Like a painting we create ourselves
Breathe shades onto our canvas of time

Hesitate, wonder, doubt … and then
Explode into the rainbow we call self

Monday Wash

She heaves her spirit onto a mountain of uncertainty
a myriad of memory piled high

The old washer wants to sigh with the weight of time,
of smiles, babies, lust and even grief

Mondays bring 3 a.m. ruminations, what not done, what not
    done enough like a lace white cloth she wants to cover thoughts
    with denial

Sheets on the line throw down tears of both joy and sadness
As her cross-wise heart wanders into remembrance

Treasured moments of warmth and safety
Traded away for a promise — when do we deliberately see?

Untold tales washed open, not quite rinsed clean of forgiveness
"Count sheep like diapers," she whispers, hold on until tomorrow's
    light.

This woman doesn't want Monday.

The Hummingbird Tree

It's up there, on the berm,
its spiky, scrubby-shrubbed,
live oak leaves
vibrate
on knobby-kneed branches.

Flittering hummingbirds
hover,
then take flight
from a springboard oak twig here,
dive bombing
from an offshoot there.
They launch themselves again and again,
trembling, vibrating, fluttering,
heat lightning fast.

The sparkle of early morning
challenges my view to perceive
pointed leaves,
windblown by strong gusts,
from tiny pronged beaks
as they become one
with the prickly branches.

The shifting, viridian foliage
shimmers up and down,
back and forth.
Leaves glisten in the morning heat
in a kind of reflective dazzle from tiny feathered bodies,
until
nectar, pregnant with sweetness,
calls from a nearby flower.

forgive us

forgive us our bypasses
shortchanges and malfeasances

forgive us our desolation and confusion
our acts of despair and collusion

our love of mass distraction
deception and exclusion

our social media addiction
and our strip-mining of delusion

forgive us our drowned ideals
and lack of distinction

forgive our inadvertence
and ambivalence to mass extinction

our algorithms of outrage
and mastery of contradiction

our tendency to bend truth
two degrees towards dysfunction

forgive us our indifference
to the singular Eccentricities of beauty

and forgive us our ignorance
of the one inescapable condition
of our human circumstance:
we are not alone

it comes in a dream

in a valley of bones a lone bee
studies a lipstick red peony
with stamens like stilettos
sharp as Dali's mustache

barometers wilt, meaning warps
a crimson pomegranate
casts a heart shaped shadow
like an angel of annunciation

with all the arrogance
and humility of the artist
the mind paints dripping time
and broken things

there are poppies for lost fertility
satyr for lust
owl for uneasiness
and death

the remains of an orange fish
harden
on a white porcelain plate
in the bayonet heat

there are tiger lilies of course
tall in a flower box
carved out of porphyry

and a woman

this isn't the dream world of Botticelli
where maidens drift through blue voids
feet naked in lush grass or rising
on nacreous half shells

this takes place along the coast
of forgotten things
in a land of stone and sky
lost to mortal time

l'hiver en Paris

line of willows along the river
long limbs curve to water
parabola's delicate trajectory
yellow dipping to grey
this day of obscure light

plangent music pours from the café
I can hear the ache in it
voiced like honey over gravel
the texture of regret
I could use a little mercy now

at dusk for an instant the city glows
phosphorescent
lamps from bridges stipple
columns of golds and blues
on the silver-foil current

Paris is solemn and beautiful
in the depths of winter
pollarded trees
clipped back gardens
architecture sculpted in faint light

space opens between things
branches blunt and bare
birds thin in the air
distant clouds adrift
moonless above the Seine

empty of summer embraces
in this deserted hour
we all could use a little mercy now

Upon reading Dylan Thomas and opening a trap door in my mind

cartwheel extravaganzas
luminescence stitched
from echoes of desire
and unmoored memories
full of premonition and wonder

mysterious metaphoric
we sail the night in dreams
myth and memory entwine
I have your face you have mine
we aren't us and we don't mind

we float over a hieroglyphic city
jigsaw of stones and tumbling skies
birds fly ellipses and strew syllables
over a dark wind-fretted
silver-maned rocking-horse sea

preoccupied with its own
immensities
and small engagements
it folds and batters
the clattered clay pebbled shore

scatters a sodality of gulls
and their affiliates
who scramble and flee
nimble in a scree
of antonyms and synecdoche

we fly over forests strung
with bluebottles and bees
leaves lusciously lissome
in strawberry breeze
the Milky Way smells

of bergamot and cheese
it's a scientific fact
tome and treatise-backed
not some mitochondrial
hack or spindly spun-off

synaptic whim
some stars smell like
a middle school gym
plimsoles and palimpsests
prepubescent and peri-adolescent

claustrophobic
and claustral
highly aerobic
explosive
and evanescent

the moon is mottled and blue
surrounded by moth-eaten clouds and rue
everything is real and nothing is true
bird on a brain wire
incantations of light

exploding prayer wheels
and something like wind chimes
with iridescent eels
spinning apostolic gleeful
maelstroms of mind

uncorked and flying free
unspooling this euphoric
mezzo mythic polymorphic
whizz bang spree
definitely no more Dylan for me!!!

on wings of osier and wax

circling a finely
calibrated thought
bright budded in morning light

in one stroke
I span the world
without predicates

buoyant in shivery air
parsing density and uplift
as easy as breath

Archon of winds
and moon pulled tides
rushing rivers

and valleys
of fire
that burn molten

on self-made wings
of osier and wax

barefoot in revolving skies
unspun from words
or human limits

far far above
the calamitous town
with its ports and bays

curves and edges
and hollows of things
that gleam at night

long necked boats
people consumed
by small pursuits

oblivious to rumor
of wings moving through
air's immensities

towards that hot
unyielding orb
at caterwauling noon

in a bell of light
birds plummet
from the sky

a boat of broken things
sails through
bone white waves

hearing the hungering
shouts of children
of gulls

sun singed
I drop
into a gold lit
swallowing sea

Lost

I knew where I was
a second ago
where I was going
and why

That was before the
fog swallowed me whole
 left me suspended
in a
place I didn't know
 my perception so altered
I became part of

Everything
and
Nothing

Between Two Worlds

You see me one way but I'm another.
Between these two worlds I walk a tightrope
Praying that again today I may cope.

You see a party girl not a mother
Struggling to ascend the higher slope.
You see me one way but I'm another.
Between these two worlds I walk a tightrope.

I know what I must do not to smother
And there are times when I appear to grope
And yet I manage to hold tight to hope.
You see me one way but I'm another.
Between these two worlds I walk a tightrope
Praying that again today I may cope.

My Guardian Angels

My guardian angels have no wings. They have four paws on strong legs, and wear thick sleek fur for warmth while racing through the cosmos like the long-distance runners they must be. My guardian angels have tall pointed ears that turn 180 degrees with white fur bursting from them to capture the songs of the cosmos from every direction without missing a beat.

My guardian angels have intense green eyes that shine with eternal unconditional love and protection for me. They have the markings of wild raccoons for their own added safety while they watch over me. My guardian angels are, in themselves, wild still, now and forever.

They have faces that express tenderness, joy, playfulness, and deep untamed wisdom. When they are at peace and content, the sides of their strong loving mouths turn upward, creating a facial expression of joyful approval. If they sense danger or another serious alert, their entire facial expression changes to intense vigilance. Their strong bodies evaluate the situation.

I can see and feel their faces preparing to take protective action to assure my safety and survival. My guardian angels fill my blessed life with the deepest love and gratitude I've ever known. They always let me know they are there by dropping a feather at my feet, filling me with immeasurable strength and assurance or by singing their next commandment LOUD and CLEAR, While my world is asleep, dreaming of peace and quiet.

My guardian angels are my closest friends for all of time eternal. They have wonderful names.Names which are their very own, which they each suggested I give them. They are The Gato, The Monya and The Moses.

They are my guardian angels...
forever.

Givers

Born like the rest of us
and raised like you and me,
they form a group apart
who mend here, there and everywhere.

These women (yes, most of them are)
never get tired of mending
what Nature in her busy plan
forgot before the final touch.

Neglected children, the needy,
sick, elders and the abused
attract and move them
to answer their inner call.

What motivates them?
The rest of us may ask.
If so, there's no need of response,
other than following their moving on.

Yes, I've met them, and so do you.
That's why these lines
bring nothing new at all.
Just memories ... plus a smile or two.

The Northern Light

The North Sea at times
forgets it's earthly bound
and lets the witness feel
what Heaven is all about.

Norway, the closest shore,
is well below the horizon
and the whole cosmos becomes
the joint of two blues: under and above.

Not for long, though.
Something begins to grow.
Is it just light and color
or beginning and end combined?

Whatever its nature is,
the witness wonders no more.
All what matters now
is being part of Beginning and End at once.

Dante's face and descriptions
become part of the experience,
which makes the witness grateful
for being one of the chosen few.

Yellowstone Dynamic

Land of random eruptions
Earth churns her discomfort
Spills her bowels upon its desolate belly
Silently nurtures her saplings
As they compete for sustenance
In the wake of charred ancestral bones
Strewn along rocky mountainsides
Monuments of eternity
Sentinels of being

Her valleys offer Aspen
Whose leaves of gold in Fall
Compete with verdant pine
Elk and eagle thrive in this majestic park
As we, cloaked in robes of mortality
Inhale the bliss of canyons
Sheltering lakes and streams
Wander-scape across her bosom
Wondering

Until the Silence

Write verse like chapter, chapter verse
Words float on rafters of mindfulness
Stung by life's turbulence
Shaped by its stillness
We go on

Travelers on seas of contemplation
Slowed when stone-strewn rivers
Create turbulent pathways
We must pursue
Until the silence
Consumes our journey
Until the silence
Becomes our goal.

My fault

My fault is hidden beneath the water,
between soft ridges covered with drought-crisped grass.

Tired tech workers come to fish on Sundays
or plough their heavy-treaded cycles into the parched earth,
breathe dust, eucalyptus, wild sage,
seek serenity.

But inside depth,
Debris from an exploding star
Was grabbed in gravity's great fist and squeezed.

Edges formed before time will not meld.
The fault shivers, the earth slides into itself,
Chews and swallows towers, bridges, highways, old-growth forests
    and gentle young hills.
Spits them out as dry ash far away.

Think you're tough?
Think you're clever?
Think you're safe?

You know nothing
About my fault.

Waitress

I remember
Picking yellow-brown foam
From cracked red vinyl seats.
"Leave that alone,"
My mother said.
Mottled grey linoleum,
Salt shaker clogged with damp salt,
Drizzle congealed on the dirty window
Between me and the fretful ocean.
Dead fly on the windowsill,
Scent of fish and rancid oil.
"It stinks in here," I said.
"Ssshhhhh!" Mother said.
Dry blond hair stiffly curled,
White frilled apron and matching headband,
White-laced shoes
Worn at the heel, thick with polish.
Freckled fingers, worn gold band.
With order pad and stubby yellow pencil,
Pretending to smile,
She looks at the water,
And waits.

Kachemak Bay

I

The mountains are shedding.
Gentle white cloaks slip off shoulders of pointed stone.
Sharp ridges and rough planes
Will scrape off human skin, let the blood out.
There will be no soft edges in the summer
Just raw bones.

II

My sister stands on the deck and waves.
The boat pulls away.
Incoming tides bring dead fish,
chunks of Styrofoam,
softening glass and pollen.
Outgoing tides take grass, dandelion seeds, wet feathers.

My sister stands on the dock and waves.
Too far now to see the tears.
Ever smaller, now hidden
by masts, breakwater,
curving earth.

Falling Asleep

Textures of blinds and blankets appear
On the other side of vision.
Stay awake and one more time rehearse
Confrontations
Missed deadlines
Unwashed dishes.
Wild plants march through the garden.
In one corner of twilight,
Paint tubes explode.
Worms of turquoise, lime and scarlet cross the mottled grey palette.
A door opens on a closet of bleached skeletons yammering.
My tiny son, in a food-spattered hand-knit Nordic sweater,
Bare-assed,
Walks out the door and disappears among the gypsies camped
    around the house.
I grope for him beneath the blankets
Find only his stepfather's knee.

Bordeaux 1969

In those days we spoke constantly about death,
Late at night, through the blue haze of Gauloise cigarettes in dank
    French rooms
Having already talked about sex, professorial quirks,
Social ills that we alone could cure.

Was it the horror on our fathers' faces
Silent, lips pinched together as they dug rocks out of the forest
Built the garden walls in new subdivisions,
Started when we came running up, squealing and squabbling
Shouted at us to go away, get away.
Was it their unspoken memories of exploding heads
The sudden eruption of a buddy's face
The blown-off hand that just a moment before had clapped them
    on the shoulder.
Could we, like little syringes, have drawn this from their sealed minds
While they bent over drawing boards late at night
Sketching Frigidaires, TV sets, washing machines,
Slicing letters from sheets with a sharp blade
Pasting them ever so carefully in place,
Preparing ads for the weekend paper.
Were we born with their memories imprinted on our minds
Or did we sense the longer, deeper horror of history

For in those days how could we have known
We, who grew in the sunshine
Of new school buildings, electric stoves, record players, Disneyland,
That love would not come soon or last long.
But we smoked and talked constantly of death.

What She Says

Her breasts were taken
and they gave her chemo
when her husband fell dead
on the half-tide beach
I still say Yes to life she says
        although ...

She talks the tautology
of give-and-take as she goes on
We're given only what we can handle
If handling is suffering
what's given could be taken back
        except that ...

The god she talks to,
a metaphor, has no ears
The only heaven is on earth
so *It takes courage to go on*
she says, the glass half full
        however ...

Everything happens for a reason
she says, that's life on earth
Rocks erode to glass on a beach
where we zigzag to take
the waves in our hands
        and yet ...

Moon Rabbit Answers

Where is what is holy

> Flush hidden pictures from the camouflage
> Put a face on the cold metallic moon

Who can say *ineffable*

> Name the gods stuck to your sole
> Give them the names of the kids next door

How do I go beyond me

> Twist your sinews from space-time
> Gather yourself at a black hole's bottom

Where on earth does the time go

> Build a temple for the space it displaces
> Simulate sky with frescoes of air

Why are people inhuman

> Choose a savior: anyone will do
> Free your redeemer before cast in gold

What changes after change

> See endless fullness, then put some in a box
> Smile: you cannot help it

Ready. Or Not

I'm not ready
to be the strong one
the buffer between hope
and the reality of now

never ready
for the wind to blow
from a new direction,
the compass held in a trembling palm.

I brush her hair
silvery weightless strands
that rest on shoulders
skeletal thin beneath her gown

massage warm oil onto her leg
cool and motionless under my hands
strength that fails her
each time she stands.

I watch the grey
creep from her hair to face
feel her pain
coil snakelike in my calf

it cuts through sleep
a burning blade slicing
through muscle
as my eyes open in anguish

unable to breathe
and the fever begins
boils in my blood
the pool of sweat

soaking my pillow
silk clinging to skin
a second layer
that shivers.

This isn't the time
for me to go down
folded in fetal sleep
lost in dream.

I stay up; she sleeps
until the air leaves the room
clocks ticking ticking
and my fever finally breaks.

Summers Ghost

The ghost of summer
haunts the trees
circles round and round each trunk
taunts them in a whispered breeze
until the sun sinks low
then lower still
its silken warm caress
now a bony chill of night
that scratches along the shivering limbs.

Each leaf in tenuous hold
will find its end
and fallen
find the artist's eye
in burnished gold and crimson
brushed too quickly
on a palette of dark, damp earth.

Caught

Each thought
is washed in a tumble
stretched out in morning sun
and dried until stiff,
pliable as I bend them
still warm in the afternoon.

I wrap each thought around my brain
as I iron them smooth
a quiver of expectation
as each word flees
and a slow sly smile curves up
to catch them from certain escape.

A Thousand Laughing Butterflies

my father spoke the language of laughter
quieting the whisper of childhood demons
to create an amusement park of diversion
a Ferris wheel of escape

mother's mirthless laugh was almost never heard,
contained, cut in the middle of release,
hidden behind obstinately closed lips
perhaps to affirm her misery
or to highlight his simplicity

much of what my mother taught me
had to be unlearned, most arduous
to reconstruct my father
with more compassion, less blame

to remember his raucous belly jiggling
lusty lawless laughter
until it hurt,
and to summon unspoken gratitude
for those stolen moments
of remission in the murk

laughing with my father was the
shortest distance we ever got to each other
an awkward expression of love even if
the intensity and length of our laughter
revealed the depth of our helplessness

today I want the sound of purging laughter,
sometimes bringing me to tears with
little concern for what was funny,
to give rise to the flight of a thousand
laughing butterflies, somewhere in the world
and whisper to my father all I never said

Jo Ann Smith

Life Throws Curveballs

it's not always a walk in the park
or fat fastballs down the middle,
sometimes life throws curve balls
with a crooked bead on your heart
throwing you off balance with the unexpected,
confusing, thwarting, outwitting

a crazy curve ball,
a deceptive spinning elliptical orb
its advance smooth and slow
before a sudden dramatic break
diving down rapidly as it approaches the plate
dropping into the strike zone like a bomb

from the trajectory of Candy Cummings
snapping seashells on Coney Island beach
to its place as intelligent idiom
this dark art pitch separates
the mimic from the eminent,
the good from the great,
the ready or not

step up to the plate
measure the speed, read the spin and
quiet the din of the crowd,
you knew it was coming
a veering vexing curve ball closing in
on your make-or-break bulwark of readiness

The Cellar Door

she was too beautiful for this place
too young for this work
too tired to ever feel young again

her workplace was the cellar,
crowded and noisy
that opened off the alley where
dirty clothes came in, clean clothes went out
the crown-jewel Maytag all that stood
between her and the poorhouse

there was an entrance to the house
off the level street directly into the living room,
three floors above the cellar,
but only company used that entrance
and though company rarely came,
she kept the second-hand furniture
carefully covered with plastic and
protected her prized imported carpet
from all inapposite passage

she endured the agitation from the men
denied access to the living room,
directed instead to descend
grudgingly to the alley
to the cellar door
to retrieve their white starched shirts,
the best she could do was sweep the
spider webs out of the open staircase

so far from the village where she grew up,
memories of her mother and the other women
laughing together, washing clothes by hand
in the Mediterranean Sea

they didn't have a Maytag, and yet ...

Under a Blanket of Dark

the colors in my room are black and
infinite shades of gray
breached only by a dot of light,
green - from the unseen cable box

sleepless, I imagine
the faint outline of the overhead fan
could be the descent of an apocalyptic demon,
the awful shadow of some sinister power
seen and gone and seen again
threatening a return to an isolated ignorance

balanced on the precipice of a familiar fall,
my eyes shut tight against such apparitions,
I seek asylum from sweet company in the dark:
faint humming from a source of power,
coyote calls from far away, nocturnal choirs
chanting in recurrent verse, the wind
just enough to usher jasmine
through my open window

blind bewildered moths,
compelled by the dark to forego their
frantic frenzy toward light,
are quietly grounded on the walls,
at rest in the welcome darkness

in symbiotic harmony
on my side of the world
the earth obscures the sun tonight
leaving the moon turned off,
at rest in a dark night sky

securely wrapped in a blanket of night
enlightened and calmed by moth and moon
my breathing part of a shadow symphony,
at rest in the paradoxical dark

Jo Ann Smith

She Brings Rhythm to My Blues

there she was,
dazzling as a fireworks finale, and
as light draws even a blind moth
I was drawn to her

no one else in that room full of people
only she, a stranger from the North, seducing me
with fantasies of an unfamiliar world
her mind like an open fire

I, a child of the moon,
fell in love with her dragon ways
her intoxicating mystery of freedom
once believed beyond my reach

the trickle found its way to river,
the fog of a foregone destiny lifted
and the haunt of the past began to vanish
as a nightmare left behind at dawn

we remain as different as melody from verse
yet merged like a rainbow's striations,
life is a continuous popping of corks
a never empty glass of bubbling Prosecco

she is the chocolate to my scotch
the poignant passion in a minor chord
she brings rhythm to my blues
she has always been my one

When words fail . . .

I return to the simple
forms of expression
that provide relief
from loss and depression.

I rumble and rattle
bark and moan
whimper and growl
to set the right tone

for what once was said
can now be sounded
a range of emotion clear,
not confounded.

Growls serve me well
when store clerks just shirk
unhelpful with questions
and only a smirk.

Speechless at the news
I've taken to sound
scream and howl
cacophony abounds.

When words fail through
memory's blur and
sentences and phrases
no longer endure
I do not fret or
wonder about dementia
the sounds that I make,
simply words in absentia.

Lost in Transition

How does it start
this shift toward the end?
Is it the low cost burial solicitation
or that hype from the crematory?

Plan now for then
don't waste a moment
do it while you can
get a deal on your demise.

I tear the ads in half, then quarters
scatter them in the recycling
ramp up my exercise routine
revisit the list of supplements.

At 50, I railed against
the invitation to join AARP,
ingest that sad newsletter about
scams, sensible shoes, senility.

Now 70, I absorb the glossy magazine
heed the health warnings and
the brightly worded guidelines
about longevity.

In the shower
I consider leaping
over the rim of the tub
in a burst of resolve when

an ad plays in my head,
"I've fallen and I can't..."
seem to find what I did
with my towel.

Laughing loudly,
I recover the towel
step out of the tub
find myself in another day.

Late Afternoon

I feel the distance between then
and when my time will come,
the end nearer than the beginning.

Decisions informed by years remaining
a cost benefit formula
for most anything.

The new carpet purchased will last
what's left of this lifetime,
the mid-century sofa affirms decades of days spent.

Futuristic predictions about global warming
water shortages, the earth's viability
trigger a quick count of how many tomorrows.

No platitude or bumper-sticker
changes the truth at the edge of mortality
life drops away in free fall to what's next.

I take comfort in a stand of redwoods outside my window
reaching for light, nurtured by fog
to simply be what I am becoming.

On Return

He no longer
dons
crisp
white t-shirts

His hair
mimics
parched
cracked
spaghetti

Loose soil
of earth
clutches the
bottom of
his
unraveled Pants

Fifteen years old
someplace,
nowhere,
everywhere,
anywhere
Where was
my
son

He's evaporated
into
the river of
adolescence

merged into
ocean

Craft your ship
rustle up your sails
make up, put up, cobble,
and
knock

Stumble over
sorrow, lost love, envy
and hate
laughter, resentment, pleasure,
indulge

When all is done
polished, buffed,
rubbed, and
lacquered

Relax your
sails
and
return
from the sea

This Is Not Jackie Collins' Bed

To sleep in sheets of Egyptian cotton
and not roll over on three senior four-legged critters
To breathe the scent of eucalyptus oil
instead of non-shampooed dachshunds
To wake in the morning with a hunk from the cover of a romance
     novel
not a hound's bum
My right arm flops over three mounds, my body launched to the far
left side of the bed, my other arm hangs midair like a dangling
     participle
To spend an afternoon meandering through Victoria secret
instead of some big-box store, loading paper towels and Clorox
     wipes into
a deranged shopping cart
To not shuffle through the herd at 2:00 am
for fear of falling and taking us all out
One by one, by one, by one
They will leave this earth and I will long
for the smell of a
freshly opened plastic container of
Clorox wipes

Fade

Only in my dreams
Do you
Appear
Leaving your smile
A trace of
Sandalwood aftershave

Arms that
Sheltered thirty years
Of love,
Tornados,
Laughter that struck from
Lightning

Blue eyes cradled by thumb printed glass
Cold silver
Frame

Your voice rests on leaf's edge
Soon to be carried away by the
Quick breath
Of
Wind

I toss words
To heaven
Like a five-year-old
Who didn't get her way

Our time together
A half-finished
Novel

Pain that once took up
Residence
In
Cracked
Heart
Now drifts to back
Rooms

I reach for the
Soft hand
Balance
Extends

Before voice drifts to sea,
Before the
Bottle traps
Your
Scent and
I no longer
Remember the straw
Stubble on your cheek

Exotic, Erotic Guava

This ceremonial banquet of
Blushed pink,
Round,
Egg,
Pear-shaped
Guava

Sink your teeth in
And
Let it
Slide through lips
Journey down throat

This forbidden fruit
From
Philippine mythology

Pink guava is what you should
Share with your lover
Or
A frozen guava and passionfruit
Popsicle that
Melts
Faster than your tongue
Can capture
Liquid drops

Stir, boil, simmer
Mash it raw
And spread
This perfumed
Confiture
Sliver thin

A pinch of chaat masala, red chili powder
Taste while
Almost
Ripe
But not quite
There yet

The evocative aroma
Will visit you
While tangled in satin sheets
Rise to the clouds

Beware though,
The softer the guava, the sweeter

But,
They go so, so bad
In about two days.

A Day Without a Name

(inspired by John Donahue)

She sat with the day
that had no name
and thus an unknown
open to anything
she brought to it

The shape of a house
trimmed in white
The Bay tree and Oak
standing silently

An elder man measuring
a board in his backyard
a story could be spun

She wanted the stillness
of a pond or a swan at rest

She wanted the roots of the Oak
and the leaves of the Bay
that hardly moved in the breeze

The day offered her silence
since it had no name
Yet her mind runs a marathon
pulling the weight
of "to do" thoughts
sitting heavily on her shoulders

A stream of lists behind her
Uncertain if she held the reins
or if the reins held her

Corlene Van Sluizer

Death Is a Drum Beat Away

Death is a drum beat away
and then there are those of us
that are left making sounds

Pressing our feet against the earth
in rhythm

When will it be my turn
and your turn and yours

Which stanza
which rest stop on the
composer's musical sheet

Will the finale be with accompaniment
a Timpani roll
or will it be the silence
after the last drum beat

Beats

Time, brazen thief
The tick-tock count down
Beats of my life
Beats of my days.

It doesn't matter now.
Silence, rage, song, cries,
Nesting in one another
Gone
But for scratchy memories,
Fingerprints on the wall,
Stains on the rug.

You left a sea of wishes
Drips in the tub
The house's heart in
The rhythm of your scent
You tapped time on the table.

The trembling, tentative now
Gone.
Bone is ashes, skin is ashes.

I hold fast to your fading words
As they sprout into stories.
Tendrils weave fragile pieces
Fleeing the cluttered past
Into memories born solid.
Beats of my life,
Beats of my days.
Tick-tock always clock.

Appendices

Poet Biographies

Judy Anderson lives in the town where she was born, these days meandering between the Bay Area and the Trinity wilderness where she builds rock sculptures, bakes pies, and dances with her muse at the river's edge. Her poems have been published in more than 15 anthologies and journals.

Barbara Armstrong, a dedicated disciple of the Blue Moon poetry salon in Sonoma County, was recognized as a merit poet in the 2017 Redwood Writers Poetry Anthology. She contributed to *Reverberations,* an ekphrastic collaboration between artists and poets. She has a lifelong fascination with the nuanced influence of words.

Marlene Augustine-Gardini retired from the music industry as Senior Director of West Coast Promotion. She is active in animal rescue; a gardener and hot air balloon enthusiast; a knitter and an actor. She has had pieces ("The Doe" and "Weight") accepted in the last two Redwood Writers anthologies; won First Place in the 2018 Memoir Contest with "The Yard" and had her piece "The Doe" featured in the 2019 California Writers Club *Literary Review.*

Stephen Bakalyar had a diverse writing career as a chemist, producing marketing materials and publishing research papers in scientific journals. He writes poetry, memoirs, essays and short stories. Subjects range widely, from the nature of water to the history of astronomy. Stories often concern the quandaries of older men.

Judy Baker is curious, compassionate and collaborative. A diet of books and healthy food, sprinkled with music, with a dash of mischief sustains her. Judy is a wellness warrior, speaker, author and book marketing mentor. She provides book marketing solutions to introverted authors.

Margaret Barkley is a poet, teacher, and curious observer of humans and nature. She has led a writing group in her home since 1999. She has an MA in Psychology with a focus on group facilitation and has taught at SSU in the Psychology Department and Organization Development Masters Program.

Warren Bellows lives and writes his poetry in West County. He is also a healer, author and visual artist. For more information see www.wbellows.com and www.floralacupuncture.com.

Jory Bellsey is a writer of poetry, short stories and op-ed pieces. He draws inspiration from music and their lyrics. He is in awe of people's ability to create art in any form. He continues to hone his skill and evolve as a writer though he still writes for the sheer joy of it

Henri Bensussen is a poet whose poems and stories have appeared in *Eclipse, Blue Mesa Review, Sinister Wisdom,* and others, and in the anthologies, *Beyond the Yellow Wallpaper: New Tales of Madness,* and *Golden State 2017*, Lisa Locasio, ed. Her chapbook of poems *Earning Colors* was published by Finishing Line Press in 2015. She has a BA in Biology. Her poems are based on the natural world and her own experiences.

Les Bernstein has poems that have appeared in journals, presses and anthologies in the U.S.A. and internationally. Her chapbooks *Borderland, Naked Little Creatures* and *Amid the Din* have been published by Finishing Line Press. Les is a winner of the 6th annual Nazim Hikmet Festival. She also was a Pushcart Prize Nominee for 2015. Les has been the editor of Redwood Writer's anthologies for 2018, 2019 and 2020 and also the editor of the Marin High School Anthology 2018.

Skye Blaine writes memoir, fiction, and poetry, developing themes of aging, coming of age, disability, and awakening. Her novel *Unleashed* was released in 2017. The sequel *Must Like Dogs* comes out in 2020. *Bound to Love: a memoir of grit and gratitude* has won three prizes including two firsts.

Laura Blatt's poems have appeared in *Lilith, California Quarterly,* Redwood Writers 2019 Poetry Anthology *Crow* and other poetry collections. She has worked as a website writer, a laboratory technician, and a publishing company manager. A member of the California Bar, Ms. Blatt also has a master's degree in biology.

Abby Lynn Bogomolny is editor of the anthology *New to North America: Writing by U.S. Immigrants* and the author of the poetry collection *People Who Do Not Exist.* Originally from Brooklyn, New York, she's lived in the SF Bay Area since the 80s. When she isn't writing, organizing, or teaching English at Santa Rosa Junior College, she can be found happily making art and music.

Catharine Bramkamp is a former professor and current writing coach, bringing her clients from idea to published book to promotion. She produced 200 episodes of the writing podcast, Newbie Writers Podcast. She has written 17 novels and 3 books on writing. Her poetry has been included in over a dozen anthologies including the chapbook *Ammonia Sunrise* by Finishing Line Press. She served as the editor for Redwood Writer's first poetry anthology, *And the Beats Go On.*

Harker Brautighan is a writer and editor in Sonoma County, California. Her previous work has appeared in the Outrider Press black-and-white anthology series, including *Falling in Love Again* and *The Moon,* in *Quill and Parchment,* and in Redwood Writers anthologies *Untold Stories* and *Endeavor.*

Robbi Sommers Bryant has award-winning books include a novella, four novels, five story collections, and one book of poetry. She is published in *Readers Digest, Redbook, Penthouse,* college textbooks, and anthologies—Robbi's work was optioned for TV's Movie of the Week. She has discussed her work on TV's Jane Whitney Show. Robbi's editing business: robbibryant.com

Marilyn Campbell draws on her experience as a former social worker when she writes. In addition to publishing two historical fiction novels, *Trains to Concordia* and *A Train to Nowhere*, she contributed poetry to *Stolen Light*, Redwood Writers 2016 Poetry Anthology. Her short stories have appeared in small journals and anthologies. She is a member of both Redwood Writers and Napa Valley Writers.

Simona Carini was born in Perugia, Italy, and moved to California as an adult. Her poetry, memoir and food writing are published in several venues. She lives in Northern California with her husband and works as an academic researcher in Medical Information Science. Her website is https://simonacarini.com

Fran Claggett-Holland, poet, editor, and inveterate teacher, is working with her favorite poetry and editing partner Les Bernstein on *And Yet,* their third Redwood Writers poetry anthology. She recently celebrated her ninetieth birthday and fourth book of poetry, *The Consciousness of Stone.* A lifelong teacher at many levels, Fran has published a number of educational books as well. She continues to write, along with the poets who gather at her home each week to share their work and their lives. Her Saluki and Whippet insist on attending these poetry sessions; they are not to be excluded from the greatest of the literary arts.

Roger DeBeers Sr., BA, History SFSU, MA English and MFA Creative Writing Goddard College. His varied background as a college English instructor, commercial pilot, flight instructor, government functionary, househusband, single custodial father, lay about, remodeling contractor, Red Diaper Baby, Street Kid, Marine Corps corporal and Army Officer lends richness to his writing.

Patrice Deems is a native Californian who just began taking dozens of spiral notebooks out of the closet in 2017, when she joined the Santa Rosa Redwood Writers. Years of poetry, song lyrics, stories, family limericks and obituaries crowd the pages. There is even an "original" musical—ten years in-the-making amongst them. No going back now!

Nancy Cavers Dougherty is a writer and artist who advocates on issues relating to child and family welfare. Nancy is the author of three chapbooks: *Tape Recorder On, Memory In Salt, Levee Town* and a collaborative work, *Silk*. She and her husband live in Sebastopol, California.

Anita Erola is a bilingual dual citizen who is originally from Finland. Her poetry and memoirs have appeared in the Finnish North American Literature Association's Journal, *Kippis* (Cheers), and in numerous anthologies. Her memoir, *Columbus Elementary School*, appears in Redwood Writers 2019 Anthology, *Endeavor*. Anita's poetry and photography have won awards.

Rebecca Evert is a member of Rumi's Caravan, a Bay Area oral tradition poetry performance group. She considers writing and memorizing poetry an essential part of her spiritual life. Rebecca is an urban farmer and an avid propagator of bee and butterfly gardens.

Robin Gabbert is a retired attorney who wrote poetry during her early years and has returned to it now that time allows. She lost her work in Tubbs Fire and is starting anew from scratch and memory. Her ideal is to "capture the essence" of a feeling, event, or scene in a few well-chosen words.

Jeff Goldman is a native Californian. Born in Monterey, raised in the Bay Area, a history graduate of Cal State Hayward, Jeff moved to Sonoma county from Sausalito in 1990. He loves Sonoma County.

Cristina Goulart writes contemporary fiction, historical fiction and poetry. Her prose and poetry have appeared in several Redwood Writers anthologies and in the California Writers Club literary magazine. Two of her short stories have been featured in Lucky Penny Productions theater events in Napa, California.

Alan Gould is a retired attorney now representing veterans in disputes with the government, has published a novel and book of short stories.

Chlele Gummer was birthed in Woodland, California 82 years ago. As a kid she joined 4H and learned to sew, to cook and to garden. In high school she took art classes. She attended Sacramento State to get a teaching credential. She married and had a daughter and a son. When they were in school she returned to teaching. After retiring she moved to Santa Rosa and soon published her first children's book, *A Family of Geese,* fully illustrating it. Since then she has written and illustrated ten other stories featuring Rufus, the Canadian gosling.

Susan E. Gunter has published poems in America, Bulgaria, England, and Montenegro. Her poems have appeared in *Atlanta Review, Emrys, Louisville Review, Paterson Review, Poet Lore, Semaphore,* etc. In 2016 her poem "Composition for Ella" won fifth place in the *Writers Digest* poetry contest.

Karen Hayes grew up in Healdsburg, CA where she spent several formative years on the Russian River. She lives in Sonoma County and loves spending time in Fort Bragg. CA where she gets most of her writing done. Her book *Riverstone* has been published.

Pamela Heck is a writer, artist and special education teacher who writes memoir, poetry, short stories and picture books. Last summer, as an artist-in-residence in Nérac, France, she completed the layout and began illustrations for her soon to be published book, *Amazing Animals, Fun Facts from A to Z.*

Lenore Hirsch is a retired educator who writes features for the *Napa Valley Register,* poetry, and stories. Her books include her dog's memoir, *My Leash on Life*; a poetry collection, *Leavings*; and *Laugh and Live, Advice for Aging Boomers.* See lenorehirsch.com, laughing-oak.com.

Basha Hirschfeld continues to reclaim her ancient roots at the same time that she strikes out into uncharted territory, discovering her authentic voice, and finding a new tenderness and vulnerability in her self-expression. She runs a retreat center and teaches meditation. She belongs to a poetry-writing group, and has contributed to several anthologies in the Sonoma County area in the past 4 years.

Louise Hofmeister thoroughly enjoys exploring various forms and hanging out with her marvelous poet-mentors and colleagues. In addition to being aired in Redwood Writers Anthology, her poems have been picked for publication by *Truth Serum, Pure Slush* and *Gnashing Teeth.*

Jon Jackson is a retired psychiatrist living in Northern California. He is a published poet and also writes prose. He currently teaches classes about Rainer Maria Rilke and various depth psychology topics.

Mara Lynn Johnstone grew up in a house on a hill, of which the top floor was built first. She lives in California with her husband, son, and laptop-loving cats. She enjoys writing, drawing, and spending hours discussing made-up things.

Briahn Kelly-Brennan writes to make her feel, when she reads it, happy, content, satisfied, astounded, dreamy or any kind of new and wonderful emotion. She feels because life can be hard, what you pay attention to grows, so why not focus on the half of the glass that is half full.

Shawn Langwell has 27 years of sales, marketing & advertising experience in the publishing industry. In November of 2016 he published his first book *Beyond Recovery, A Journey of Grace, Love, and Forgiveness*. When he's not working or writing he can be found hiking the West Marin Coast. He lives in Petaluma with his wife Crissi and three adult children.

Betty Les has been writing poetry for most of her life although she didn't always know it. Her work explores the intersection of science and the mysteries of nature and how poetry can help make meaning of our life and times. She was chosen as a Redwood Writers Award of Merit Poet in 2018. Betty holds an MA in Zoology.

Sherrie Lovler is a painter and poet from Santa Rosa. She is an Art Trails artist and teaches Lyrical Abstract Painting locally, nationally and in France. Sherrie's paintings and poems inspire each other and are paired in her award-winning book *On Softer Ground: Paintings, Poems and Calligraphy*.

Roger C. Lubeck, Ph.D. is vice president of the California Writers Club and president of the Redwood Writers. Roger's published works include articles, seven novels, two business books, fifteen short stories and poems, two produced short plays, and two prize-winning short stories. Roger is working on a screenplay and three novels.

Mark Meierding has lived in Sonoma County since 1980. He enjoys writing poetry with a variety of styles, tones, and themes. He appreciates how poetry's unique combinations of language and imagination can help us perceive our world in new ways.

Phyllis Meshulam MFA Vermont College is the author of *Land of My Father's War*, winner of 2019 Artists' Embassy International Award, published by Cherry Grove Collections. She teaches with California Poets in the Schools. For CalPoets' 50th anniversary, she edited *Poetry Crossing*, a joyful collection of lessons and poems.

Stephanie Moore is a retired English teacher from Santa Rosa, a poet and writer. She is also a singer, most recently performing with the Sonoma Valley Chorale, and a visual artist, currently studying pastel painting. Her poetry has been published in *The Marin Poetry Center Anthology* and in *California Quarterly*.

Patricia Nelson worked for many years with the "Activist" group of poets formed and led by Lawrence Hart and then by his son, John Hart. Nelson is a retired attorney. Her most recent book is *Out of the Underworld*, Poetic Matrix Press.

Ellie Portner is a visual artist and a poet. She exhibits her artwork at the Sonoma Arts Guild in the town of Sonoma. Ellie is inspired to write poetry. Her poems have appeared in the 2018 and 2019 Redwood Writers poetry anthologies.

Linda Loveland Reid is the past president of Redwood Writers and recipient of the Jack London Award. She is author of two novels. Linda graduated cum laude with two BA degrees from SSU, and currently teaches art history for SSU and Dominican Universities through the Osher Lifelong Learning Institute. Linda is a figurative oil painter and theater director. (website: LindaLovelandReid.com)

Jane Rinaldi has a bit more confidence in her poetry writing these days; she is always amazed when there is a positive reception to it. What joy to write a pleasing poem, more exciting than reciting "Little Orphan Annie" to her grandmother's friends at age five.

Margaret Rooney is a retired psychotherapist with an addiction to writing poetry. Her poetry group helps her manage it in a positive, self-reflective way. She has published in The Redwood Writers' 2018 and 2019 Anthology, *Reverberations, Ekphrasis Journal* and has a poem nominated for the 2020 Pushcart Prize.

Janice Rowley has been in many places, from the rural South to the California wine country, from airline to veterinary, from show dogs to rescue dogs, from reading to writing, from memoir to poetry to fiction, from a young woman with dreams to an aged one with memories. Jan's prose and poetry has been published in various Redwood Writers' annual anthologies.

Dmitri Rusov-Morningstar is a ripe old hippie with good humor. During the 1960's and 70's, he worked tirelessly for peace. He became a union carpenter and has been a residential designer for the past thirty-six years. Writing is his passion. He writes memoir and stories about his Maine Coon Cats.

Luis Salvago-Toledo was born and raised in Málaga (Spain), where he attended the Merchant Marine Academy, Master. After sailing as a deck officer for over 10 years, he settled down in California. Here he worked in the computer field while studying philosophy (BA UCLA, MA UC Berkeley). Today a retiree, he enjoys tutoring Spanish and occasionally writing newspaper columns.

Florentia Scott has poetry that explores connections and disconnections between concrete reality and imagination. Her work has appeared in the *Alberni Valley Times, Ascent Aspirations Magazine*, the 2009 San Francisco Writer's Conference Anthology and the 2018 and 2019 Redwood Writers poetry anthologies.

Jan Seagrave has poems that have appeared in Marin Poetry Center Anthology 2016 and 2017; Redwood Writers Poetry Anthology 2018 and 2019; *Amore: Love Poems*, ed. J. Tucker; and *Herself: A Portrait*. She attended Bread Loaf Writers Conference in 1979 and earlier won the top high school award of CA Chaparral Poets.

Alicia Schooler-Hugg is a former op-ed columnist and features writer for *The (Stockton) Record, Modesto Bee, Nurseweek* and Nurse.com. As a registered nurse, she taught university level communications courses and received several journalism-based awards. She has authored two books: *Art and Soul of Jazz: A Tribute to Charles Mingus, Jr.*, and *Granny Does Europe: A Love Story*.

Robert Shafer is the author of *Mickey: The Giveaway Boy*, grew up as a Chicago slum boy and abandoned child. He served 1960-64 in the US Navy and worked thirty-five-years as a film/video editor in San Francisco. His childhood experiences inspire much of his writing. He resides in Napa, CA.

Nancy Sharp has always seen the world through words that flow as freely as an artist applies color to a canvas. It may be that poets are born with the creative desire to express themselves using poems to tell their story. She certainly believes this to be true.

Jo Ann Smith spent most of her life in public education as a teacher, counselor, principal and for the last twelve years superintendent, all at the high school level. In those capacities she relied most on the orderly left side of her brain. Now retired, she finds herself drawn to the evocative nature of poetry, achieved through imagery, scene, tone of voice and a very different kind of writing specificity. This journey continues to be challenging, revealing and liberating. In 2019 Jo Ann was recognized with an "award of merit" and had five poems published in Redwood's poetry anthology, *Crow*.

Linda Stamps established careers in law, journalism, and higher education. Her published works include poetry, fiction, and nonfiction. She is a member of the Blue Moon Salon and Redwood Writers. Her poetry is inspired by a phrase here, a word there, and the rhythm of the heart.

Kathleen Torian Taylor has a Bachelor of Arts from the University of the Pacific. She is a member of Gini Grossenbacher's Amherst Writers & Artists California State Legislation Certificate of Recognition, Stockton Arts commission, She has an Honorable Mention, Soul Making Literary Prize. Her poetry is published in *Haight Ashbury Literary Journal, Lazer, Melodies of the Soul,* The National Library of Poetry, *Prophetic Voices.*

Corlene Van Sluizer self published *Resurgence*, a poetry book. Each poem is illustrated with her original artwork. Her poetry has been published in many newsletters and publications such as: *A Moving Journal, Business World* and *Pegasus Journal* and an article in *The Journal of Dance and Somatic Practices* on "Art and Poetry in Authentic Movement."

Marilyn Wolters has lived in Sonoma County for over forty years. She spent most of her working years helping disabled college students develop essay-writing skills. Now retired, she can't resist writing regularly. Her poetry, short stories and short plays have been published and performed.

Artists' Statements

Linda Loveland Reid loves to paint the female, from her curves to the inner spirit of mom, wife, lover and nuturer. Mixed together these attributes evoke life, mystery and complex feelings that emerge through the canvas. I want my women to be unmasked and rid of the apple-syndrome. Age-wise, they have a bit of life behind them, lessons learned, regrets massaged. I draw only to paint, probably because rendering is not a natural skill for me. Actually neither is painting. One day after being the devoted voyeur for many years, Harry bought me a set of water colors, sat me down, set up the canvas, put a brush in my hand and said, "Just do it." That was in 1986. This year, I've burst into abstract work and am loving it. Painting is peace when it isn't terrifying.

Rebecca Smith has loved to paint since her mother, an artist, wrapped her up in one of dad's old oxford shirts, gave her paints and well-used brushes, and encouraged her freedom of expression at a very young age. To Rebecca, art is poetry blended into light and color - landing to create impact. Her art is a happy place of peace and discovery, as well as a visually haunting social commentary. In between shades of joy lay brush strokes of will manipulated into form by a consciousness greater than the artist's.

Redwood Branch History

Jack London was first attracted to the beauty of Sonoma County in 1909, the very year he was named an honorary founding member of the Berkeley-based California Writers Club [CWC].

In 1975 Redwood Writers was established as the fourth CWC branch, due to special impetus from Helene S Barnhart of the Berkeley Branch, who had relocated to the North Bay. She and forty-five charter members founded the Redwood Branch of the CWC.

Redwood Writers is a non-profit organization whose motto is: "writers helping writers." The organization's mission is to provide a friendly and inspirational environment in which members may meet, network, and learn about the writing industry.

Monthly meetings are open to the public and feature professional speakers who present a variety of topics from writing skills to publishing and marketing.

The club sponsors a variety of activities, such as, contests and workshops. Every other year the club holds a day-long Writers Conference, offering seminars on all areas of writing.

Redwood Writers publishes a members' anthology, now celebrating thirteen consecutive years, in addition to a Poetry Anthology, giving members an opportunity to publish their work.

In cooperation with the county's largest bookstore, Copperfield's Books, Redwood Writers presents "Hot Summer Nights," where members' books are reviewed for discussion at meetings open to the general public. Each year, club members staff a booth at the Sonoma County Fair, where books are sold and writing tips are offered to Fair attendees.

An extensive monthly newsletter and award winning website, along with other social media outlets, keeps members in touch with one another, to share accomplishments and successes.

Redwood Writers is indebted to its founders and charter members, to the leaders who have served at the helm, and to our many members. Without this volunteer dedication, Redwood Writers could not have developed into the professional club it is today with over 300 members. For more information visit *www.redwoodwriters.org.*

Redwood Writers Presidents

Redwood Branch is indebted to its founders, charter members, and to the leaders who have served at the helm, and, of course, to our many members. Without their volunteer hours and dedication to the club's mission, Redwood Writers could not have developed into the professional and successful club it is today with 300 members.

1975	Helen Schellenberg Barnhart	1992	Barb Truax (4 years)
1976	Dianne Kurlfinke	1997	Marvin Steinbock (2 years)
1977	Natlee Kenoyer	1999	Dorothy Molyneaux
1978	Inman Whipple	2000	Carol McConkie
1979	Herschel Cozine	2001	Gil Mansergh (2 years)
1980	Edward Dolan	2003	Carol McConkie
1981	Alla Crone Hayden	2004	Charles Brashear
1982	Mildred Fish	2005	Linda C. McCabe (2 years)
1983	Waldo Boyd	2007	Karen Batchelor (2 years)
1984	Margaret Scariano	2009	Linda Loveland Reid (3 years)
1985	Dave Arnold	2013	Robbi Sommers Bryant (1.5 years)
1986	Mary Priest (2 years)	2015	Sandy Baker (2 years)
1988	Marion McMurtry (2 years)	2017	Roger C. Lubeck (2 years)
1990	Mary Varley (2 years)		

Awards

Jack London Award

Every other year, CWC branches may nominate a member to receive the Jack London Award for outstanding service to the branch, sponsored by CWC Central. The recipients are:

1975	Helen Schellenberg Barnhart	1998	Barbara Truax
1977	Dianne Kurlfinke	2003	Nadenia Newkirk
1979	Peggy Ray	2004	Gil Mansergh
1981	Pat Patterson	2005	Mary Rosenthal
1983	Inman Whipple	2007	Catherine Keegan
1985	Ruth Irma Walker	2009	Karen Batchelor
1987	Margaret Scariano	2011	Linda C. McCabe
1989	Mary Priest	2013	Linda Loveland Reid
1991	Waldo Boyd	2015	Jeane Slone
1993	Alla Crone Hayden	2017	Sandy Baker
1995	Mildred Fish	2019	Robbi Sommers Bryant
1997	Mary Varley		

Helene S. Barnhart Award

In 2010 this award was instituted, inspired by Redwood Writers first president, to honor outstanding service to the branch, given in alternate years to the Jack London Award.

2010	Kate (Catharine) Farrell	2016	Robin Moore
2012	Ana Manwaring	2018	Malena Eljumaily
2014	Juanita J. Martin		

Additional copies
of this book
may be purchased at
amazon.com
and other retail outlets.

CPSIA information can be obtained
at www.ICGtesting.com
Printed in the USA
BVHW041549050420
576890BV00010B/984